IF LIFE GIVES YOU LEMONS...

IF LIFE GIVES YOU LEMONS...

HOW 10 SECONDS A DAY CAN BRING YOU HAPPINESS

SALLY STUBBS

www.sallystubbs.com

GIBSON SQUARE

First published in 2011 by

Gibson Square

Tel: +44 (0)20 7096 1100

info@gibsonsquare.com
www.gibsonsquare.com

ISBN 9781906142810

CONTENTS

At your leisure...

IF LIFE GIVES YOU LEMONS...

HOW 10 SECONDS A DAY CAN BRING
YOU HAPPINESS

This book is your travel guide to your happiness. It will travel with you, and you do not have to leave your home or office to find yourself and your true happiness.

If you have one of those bleary eyed moments in your day, those moments of feeling stuck as if you are worn down by experiencing the same thing over and over again, those indecisive moments, those mundane moments of balancing your finances, this book aims to help you with some joy in ten seconds.

Crucial to this is the power of the little word 'if'. Only two letters long, it is one of the most potent words in the English language. We all know the expression 'what if'. In a split second it will transport you from the present to an entirely different world.

However, 'if' is capable of doing many more things in less than 10 seconds, as I will show in this book.

By turning to the category of 'Ifs' that you want and need, you can uplift and enhance your mood. Choose when you want to wonder or to consider... Choose when you want to explore life, the universe, everything! Choose when you need to enhance your mood... Choose when you want to smile... Choose when you need to find a new 'angle', a solution for you... Your choice; choose one quote, a page a day...or choose five pages a day… or choose intuitively…

The quotes are like little wings to enable you, in seconds, to move to solutions, satisfaction and towards success. In only a few moments the quotes can give you essential keys to think and feel differently, act resourcefully and happily.

On a deeper level, if you have a crisis of foresight you may have feelings of being overwhelmed. The quotes will tell you that you're not alone. Most of us do have these experiences. The quotes and the real life stories of others, their difficulties, pain and fear and the great courage, and invaluable insights show they had their own 'If…' to overcome.

As you take these little wings in one by one, they will help you to come up with your important and valuable 'If…' moments where you see more clearly your own path to greater happiness.

For Mike

People and their stories

All these wonderful people, and many, many others who I deeply respect, have been a gift to me, I feel so grateful to be able to share them with you.

It is my deepest wish that these stories will perhaps play a part in you continuing to know the genius within you, and 'If' their stories do resonate with you, perhaps you will want to help bring out the genius in the people that you touch.

'If from now on you treat everyone that you meet like a holy person, you will be happy.'

— *Susan Trott (The Holy Man)*

'Ifs...'
for the 'Fire' of your heart

A tip to experience the fire of the warmth and passion in your heart...

If you are already working with a category or categories of your negative thoughts – that is the thoughts that are not celebrating or supporting life – you are already working towards the right kind of 'fuel' for the fire of warmth and passion in your heart.

The warmth of happiness in your heart is firstly 'fuelled' from your own thoughts *and* beliefs about your self and life. Perhaps you will have noticed that some of your negative thoughts are non constructive beliefs about your self? If our beliefs about our self are negative or destructive, they provide damp, soggy, useless fuel for our heart. Our negative beliefs about our self can and do create a barrier to receiving into our heart the good and positive fuel from the support or real compliments from others.

So, one thing that we, you, can do to provide the heart with good fuel is to create constructive beliefs about our self.

This isn't an ego trip. This is about validating our selves; we all need validation, and if we do not get it, or cannot take it in from others, we need to give it to ourselves.

The self-validating beliefs that I am talking about are not

necessarily about what you *do*, but are simply about who you *are*.

You are a human being with vast potential.

If we begin to give up who we believed we were, we can become who we are.

Listen for your inner beliefs about who you are – and begin to change the destructive or the negative. Make the changes with passion in your inner dialogue. Your brain will respond to the energy in your passion and will soon be unable to access the old negative beliefs. Begin to validate your self right now with positive self-reinforcing beliefs that you have. You may end up with an inner dialogue that might dispute a belief that you validate your self with. What do I mean? Here is a simple example: 'I am a kind person.' An inner dialoguing response might be: 'Ah, but you were unkind last week.' Now here is an important tip: don't argue with that part of yourself with 'Yes, but they were horrible.' Always, always respond with 'That's right, I was' and continue your dialogue with that part of yourself with: 'However I can and I will continue to learn to be kinder.' The 'That's right' response will allow the inner battle to cease. The 'That's right' response brings inner truth and peace. The true belief about who I am: 'I can and I will continue to learn to be kinder.'

My Story

If you have only one smile in you, give it to the people you love. Don't be surly at home, then go out in the street and start grinning 'Good morning' at total strangers.

— *Maya Angelou*

Can you think of a time when 'If' could have changed the entire course of your life?

I certainly can. I had a massive 'If' in 1992 which I often remember with gladness in my heart because I did not succumb to the fear that 'If' wanted me to respond to.

I had recently met an adventurous, sturdy man and fallen deeply in love.

He has strong legs and unruly misbehaving hair that falls about in all directions.

He invited me to join him for an exciting six week adventure to travel across four African countries. Just the two of us and a 4-wheel drive, all kitted out for camping, complete with winches and ropes in case we got stuck. He was ready for me to join him in the bush, to share together our awe of lions, elephants, rare wild dog and all manner of wondrous natural life, the strange; hauntingly beautiful sounds of the night; the vastness of the Namibian desert and the infinite space of the sky arcing over Botswana.

Not everyone's dream adventure, I know!

I packed my bags and as I was about to leave for the airport I suddenly felt anxious and, hastily interpreting this acute feeling, I thought, '*If* I go on this trip I will be being irresponsible! *If* I go, I will be neglecting my clients!' Filled with fear at the possibility of being negligent and overwhelmed with panic pounding in my stomach, I picked up the phone to cancel. I had almost dialled his number in Cape Town when I had the good fortune or inner wisdom to think, 'Hang on a minute! I'm not irresponsible! I've worked really hard and diligently to make sure all my clients will be comfortable, and my reception staff are happy. In fact, every one is saying go and have fun!'

I pushed my almost packed case off the bed. The flimsy new underwear and glitzy shoes, totally unsuitable for the African Bush, fell to the floor.

I lay down listening to the pounding fear in my stomach and then I heard a deep unconscious, conditioned injunction, a restricting inner dialogue: 'You can't have your cake and eat it!'

These were the words that were driving my fear and my anxiety.

These were words in my mind, all the way back from my early childhood; they came from my mother and my grandmother. They were good women, who had had some lovely cakes, but sadly they held a belief that life was too harsh to eat cake.

They had been protecting me from disappointment with their teaching: 'If you eat your cake there will be none left! You'll *never* have another cake!'

I considered a moment and my thought burst in a blaze of passion: 'Mum, Grandma, I do respect you, but what is the point in having cake and not eating it!?' I decided to eat cake, lots of delicious ones! My stomach glowed with relief. I went to Africa, I joined my man.

This is such a deeply felt experience in my life of the

extraordinary power of 'If', because, 'If' I had not gone to Africa, 'If' I had not taken time to listen to my unconscious driving thought, I would never have seen my man again.

He and I are now living together. Our love and understanding grows and flourishes, and I know that because of our love, he and I are able to assist so many others to heal troubles and wounds in their lives.

Together he and I consider my 'If'!

If and when we *do* now eat cakes, lots of them, nourishing cakes, scrumptious, fun cakes, serious cakes, the cakes that take time and effort to carefully create, we grow in our strengths and in our resources.

My man makes all kinds of great cakes.

We can bring the purity of gold to our thoughts.

We can experience the fire of the warmth and passion in our hearts.

We can digest the minerals and crystals for the strength and stability of our bones

We can take flight in the expansiveness of air to express and feel our humour, creativity and fun.

We can value the diamonds of our soul's clarity and permanence.

'If' truly is one of the most important words we use, especially in our emotional thoughts and internal dialogue. An 'If' can alter the entire course of our lives.

I will continue to bring the fire of the warmth and passion to my heart...

Michael's Story

*If we fall, we don't need self-recrimination or blame or anger —
we need a reawakening of our intention and a willingness to
recommit, to be whole-hearted once again.*

— *Sharon Salzberg*

It is many years ago that Michael came to see me. He was
then in his early seventies, a solid stocky body, a shock of
pure white hair, a gentle man, the sparkle in his blue eyes
hiding behind shifting grey, like memories of clouds in an
overcast sky.

Michael asked me if I could help him. He wanted to stop
trembling.

Ever since the war he had a trembling in his body, mostly
in his hands, and over the years it had been getting worse
and worse. He said that he had been an RAF pilot during the
war, when he was still too young to vote. He said that he
remembered the night of the bombing of the city.

He said that in his mind, in his thoughts, he believed that
the bombing was right, and in his heart he felt it was wrong.

He then became quiet for a while before he suddenly told
me a story from his childhood: 'My three-and-a-half year-
old brother Thomas died. Thomas took with him a piece of
my father's heart, to prove to the angels that he had lived his
short life on earth with a gentle man. Oh, God that I could
leave such legacy.'

He experienced the memory of the night of the bombing
as playing round and round in his mind, even when he was

not aware of it; he felt it continuously playing on and on.

The picture he had was of just before the bombs were dropped from the plane. Michael said it's as if he can still feel his parachute on his seat beneath him, he can see the pilot's instrument panel and he can see his hands shaking on the pilot's control column.

In his heart, in that moment he wants to turn the plane sharply, navigate away from the city, away from the port, fly over the sea and ditch it.

Michael cannot do so, and he does not do what his heart wants.

Michael's mind froze that moment in time, in an attempt to stop, in the next coming moments, his own death at his own hands, or the inevitable death of innocent people in the city below him.

If he carries on with the bombing mission, many thousands will die, and so, too, he deeply believes his gentle heart will perish. If he turns and ditches the plane he will die, and he will also be letting down a great courageous crew, of a brilliant ground crew, the honour of the Royal Air Force and the hopes and beliefs of the British people.

In his mind Michael takes neither action; Deep in his unconscious mind he stopped that moment in time, as the choice to let the bombs go and destroy the lives of the people of the city was unacceptable to his heart, his only other choice to ditch the plane and to damage and dishonour so many was unacceptable to his mind, beliefs and way of thinking.

How can Michael move on from that trembling, shaking moment?

He did carry on with his mission – the bombs were dropped, the extreme fires and massive loss of life happened. He knows this, yet in a way the part of him that is stuck or frozen in that time (more than fifty years earlier), does not know or does not accept what happened next.

Only Michael and his heart knew the answer how to bring some healing to those moments, suspended in time over the city.

The answer came as we carefully explored more of the information.

Michael had a realisation that since that dark night, he blamed himself, and he blamed his heart. He so often, beat his right fist over his heart and exclaimed 'Mea Culpa... Mea Culpa... Mea Maxima Culpa...' My Fault... My Fault... My Grievous Fault...

Michael had held a belief that he needed to ask God for his forgiveness, and suddenly as he spoke he realised that he actually deeply believed that God did not blame him.

Then he allowed the images that his heart had wanted, he pictured that he turned and navigated the plane, ditched over the sea, away from the city and the port, and felt his heart soar free as he imagined the plane sinking beneath the water.

The trembling and shaking had come from Michael's heart; his heart had been captured like a bird in a cage of fear, trembling for over half a century.

For the fire, warmth and passion of Michael's heart...

Quotes to continue to experience the fire of warmth and passion in your heart...

These quotes and stories will rekindle you when you are feeling disheartened, dampened down, oppressed, scared, or apprehensive.

'If...' quotes and stories for the fire in your heart will relight your enthusiasm, excitement, delight and fervour for your unique passions and loves.

'If time is money, it seems moral to save time, above all one's own, and such parsimony is excused by consideration for others.'

— *Theodor Adorno*

'If you can once engage people's pride, love, pity, ambition on your side, you need not fear what their reason can do against you.'

— *Lord Chesterfield*

'If every man's internal care Were written on his brow, How many would our pity share Who raise our envy now?'

— *Pietro Metastatio*

'If we don't see a failure as a challenge to modify our approach, but rather as a problem with ourselves, as a personality defect, we will immediately feel overwhelmed.'

— *Anthony Robbins*

'If the only prayer you ever say in your entire life is 'thank you', it will be enough.'

— *Meister Eckhart*

'If we have been pleased with life, we should not be displeased with death, since it comes from the hand of the same master.'

— *Michelangelo*

'If you love someone, set them free. If they come back they're yours; if they don't they never were.'

— *Richard Bach*

'If you can dream it, then you can achieve it. You will get all you want in life if you help enough other people get what they want.'

— *Zig Ziglar*

'If your real desire is to be good, there is no need to wait for the money before you do it; you can do it now, this very moment, and just where you are.'

— *James Allen*

'If you are right, take the humble side – you will help the other fellow. If you are wrong, take the humble side – and you will help yourself.'

— *Anonymous*

'If you aren't good at loving yourself, you will have a difficult time loving anyone, since you'll resent the time and energy you give another person that you aren't even giving to yourself.'

— Barbara De Angelis

'If you have tried to do something and failed, you are vastly better off than if you had tried to do nothing and succeeded. You must never regret what might have been. The past that did not happen is as hidden from us as the future we cannot see.'

— Richard Martin Stern

'If it's never our fault, we can't take responsibility for it. If we can't take responsibility for it, we'll always be its victim.'

— Richard Bach

'If there is anything better than to be loved it is loving.'

— Anonymous

'If you go looking for a friend, you're going to find they're very scarce. If you go out to be a friend, you'll find them everywhere.'

— Zig Ziglar

'If you have much, give of your wealth; if you have little, give of your heart.'

— *Arabian proverb*

'If you would thoroughly know anything, teach it to others.'

— *Tryon Edwards*

'If there's just one kind of folks, why can't they get along with each other? If they're all alike, why do they go out of their way to despise each other?'

— *Harper Lee (To Kill A Mockingbird)*

'If a man has no humaneness what can his propriety be like? If a man has no humaneness what can his happiness be like?'

— *Confucius*

'If thou art a man, admire those who attempt great things, even though they fail.'

— *Seneca*

'If you treat your friend as they should be, they will become one of the crowd. If you treat your friend as they ought to be treated, they will become an individual.'

— *Anonymous*

'If I had my hand full of truth, I would take good care how I opened it.'

— *Bernard Le Bovier Fontenelle*

'If any man seeks for greatness, let him forget greatness and ask for truth, and he will find both.'

— *Horace Mann*

'If there is such a thing as a good marriage, it is because it resembles friendship rather than love.'

— *Michel de Montaigne*

'If one does not understand a person, one tends to regard him as a fool.'

— *Carl Jung*

'If I am to care for people in hospital I really must know every aspect of their treatment and to understand their suffering.'

— *Princess Diana of Wales*

'If only we'd stop trying to be happy we could have a pretty good time.'

— *Edith Wharton*

'If you want to be happy, be.'

— *Leo Tolstoy*

'If your heart acquires strength, you will be able to remove blemishes from others without thinking evil of them.'

— *Mohandas K. Ghandi*

'If you would convince others, seem open to conviction yourself.'

— *Lord Chesterfield*

'If the machine of government is of such a nature that it requires you to be the agent of injustice to another, then, I say, break the law.'

— *Henry David Thoreau*

'If you want others to be happy, practice compassion. If you want to be happy, practice compassion.'

— *Dalai Lama*

'If you're not using your smile, you're like a man with a million dollars in the bank and no check book.'

— *Les Giblin*

'If there is anything that we wish to change in the child, we should first examine it and see whether it is not something that could better be changed in ourselves.'

— *Carl Jung*

'If you take responsibility for yourself you will develop a hunger to accomplish your dreams.'

— *Les Brown*

'If you believe in unlimited quality and act in all your business dealings with total integrity, the rest will take care of itself.'

— *Frank Perdue*

'If one has no affection for a person or a system, one should feel free to give the fullest expression to his disaffection so long as he does not contemplate, promote, or incite violence.'

— *Mohandas Gandhi*

'If we really think that home is elsewhere and that this life is a 'wandering to find home,' why should we not look forward to the arrival?'

— *C. S. Lewis*

'If you have not often felt the joy of doing a kind act, you have neglected much, and most of all yourself.'

— *A. Neilan*

'If you can give your son or daughter only one gift, let it be enthusiasm.'

— *Bruce Barton*

'If you wish your merit to be known, acknowledge that of other people.'

— *Oriental proverb*

'If you have love in your life it can make up for a great many things you lack. If you don't have it, no matter what else there is, it's not enough.'

— *Ann Landers*

'If you are patient in one moment of anger, you will escape a hundred days of sorrow.'

— *Chinese proverb*

'If indeed you must be candid, be candid beautifully.'

— *Kahlil Gibran*

'If you would be pungent, be brief; for it is with words as with sunbeams – the more they are condensed, the deeper they burn.'

— *John Dryden*

'If you can go through life without experiencing pain you probably haven't been born yet.'

— *Neil Simon*

'If you cannot lift the load off another's back, do not walk away. Try to lighten it.'

— *Frank Tyger*

'If I have said something to hurt a man once, I shall not get the better of this by saying many things to please him.'

— *Samuel Johnson*

'If we would build on a sure foundation in friendship, we must love friends for their sake rather than for our own.'

— *Charlotte Bronte*

'If a man does not make new acquaintances as he advances through life, he will soon find himself alone. A man should keep his friendships in constant repair.'

— *Samuel Johnson*

'If you are a terror to many, then beware of many.'

— *Ausonius*

'If there's any message to my work, it is ultimately that it's OK to be different, that it's good to be different, that we should question ourselves before we pass judgment on someone who looks different, behaves different, talks different, is a different colour.'

— *Johnny Depp*

'If we cannot live so as to be happy, let us least live so as to deserve it.'

— *Immanuel Hermann Fichte*

'If you would stand well with a great mind, leave him with a favourable impression of yourself; if with a little mind, leave him with a favourable impression of himself.'

— *Samuel Taylor Coleridge*

'If your morals make you dreary, depend on it, they are wrong.'

— *Robert Louis Stevenson*

'If you cannot work with love but only with distaste, it is better that you should leave your work.'

— *Kahlil Gibran*

'If one by one we counted people out For the least sin, it wouldn't take us long To get so we had no one left to live with. For to be social is to be forgiving.'

— *Robert Frost*

'If you hire only those people you understand, the company will never get people better than you are. Always remember that you often find outstanding people among those you don't particularly like.'

— *Soichiro Honda*

'If we escape punishment for our vices, why should we complain if we are not rewarded for our virtues?'

— *John Churton Collins*

'If liberty means anything at all, it means the right to tell people what they do not want to hear.'

— *George Orwell*

'If you cannot forgive, you cannot love without conditions.'
— *Janine Duthac*

'If you look into your own heart, you find nothing wrong there, what is there to fear?'
— *Confucius*

'If we don't know life, how can we know death?'
— *Confucius*

'If people can be educated to see the lowly side of their own natures, it may be hoped that they will also learn to understand and to love their fellow men better. A little less hypocrisy and a little more tolerance towards oneself can only have good results in respect for our neighbour; for we are all too prone to transfer to our fellows the injustice and violence we inflict upon our own natures.'
— *Carl Jung*

'If you load responsibility on a man unworthy of it he will always betray himself.'
— *August Heckscher*

'If there is something to pardon in everything, there is also something to condemn.'

— *Friedrich Nietzsche*

'If you desire to drain to the dregs the fullest cup of scorn and hatred that a fellow human being can pour out for you, let a young mother hear you call dear baby 'it'.'

— *T. S. Eliot*

'If you can't feed a hundred people, then feed just one.'

— *Mother Teresa*

'If we have no peace, it is because we have forgotten that we belong to each other.'

— *Mother Teresa*

'If we want a love message to be heard, it has got to be sent out. To keep a lamp burning, we have to keep putting oil in it.'

— *Mother Teresa*

'If we are to achieve a richer culture, rich in contrasting values, we must recognize the whole gamut of human potentialities, and so weave a less arbitrary social fabric, one in which each diverse human gift will find a fitting place.'

— *Margaret Mead*

'If all my friends were to jump off a bridge, I wouldn't jump with them, I'd be at the bottom to catch them.'

— *Anonymous*

'If you're trusted and people will allow you to share their inner garden...what better gift?'

— *Fred Rogers*

'If we discovered that we had only 5 minutes left to say what we wanted to say, every telephone booth would be occupied by people calling other people to stammer that they loved them.'

— *Christopher Morley*

'If men could only know each other, they would neither idolize nor hate.'

— *Elbert Hubbard*

'If there were in the world today any large number of people who desired their own happiness more than they desired the unhappiness of others, we could have paradise in a few years.'

— Bertrand Russell

'I shall not live in vain.'

— Emily Dickinson

'If you want to build a ship, don't drum up people together to collect wood and don't assign them tasks and work, but rather teach them to long for the endless immensity of the sea.'

— Antoine de Saint-Exupery

'If you can, help others; if you cannot do that, at least do not harm them.'

— Dalai Lama

'If all the world hated you and believed you wicked, while your own conscience approved of you and absolved you from guilt, you would not be without friends.'

— Charlotte Bronte (Jane Eyre)

'If people were always kind and obedient to those who are cruel and unjust; the wicked people would have it all their own way: they would never feel afraid, and so they would never alter, but would grow worse and worse.'

— *Charlotte Bronte (Jane Eyre)*

'If you make it plain you like people, it's hard for them to resist liking you back.'

— *Lois McMaster Bujold (Diplomatic Immunity)*

'If each man or woman could understand that every other human life is as full of sorrows, or joys, or base temptations, of heartaches and of remorse as his own...how much kinder, how much gentler he would be.'

— *William Allen White*

'If you knew what I know about the power of giving, you would not let a single meal pass without sharing it in some way.'

— *Buddha*

'If you were all alone in the universe with no one to talk to, no one with which to share the beauty of the stars, to laugh with, to touch, what would be your purpose in life? It is other life, it is love, which gives your life meaning. This is harmony. We must discover the joy of each other, the joy of challenge, the joy of growth.'

— *Mitsugi Saotome*

'If there must be trouble let it be in my day, that my child may have peace.'

— *Thomas Paine*

'If you want to make peace with your enemy, you have to work with your enemy. Then he becomes your partner.'

— *Nelson Mandela*

'If you hate a person, you hate something in him that is part of yourself. What isn't part of ourselves doesn't disturb us.'

— *Hermann Hesse*

'If you go in for argument, take care of your temper. Your logic, if you have any, will take care of itself.'

— *Joseph Farrell*

'If you want to make peace, you don't talk to your friends. You talk to your enemies.'

— *Moshe Dayan*

'If one only wished to be happy, this could be easily accomplished; but we wish to be happier that other people, and this is always difficult, for we believe others to be happier than they are.'

— *Charles De Montesquieu*

'If we could read the secret history of our enemies, we should find in each man's life sorrow and suffering enough to disarm all hostility.'

— *Henry Wadsworth Longfellow*

'If we lose love and self-respect for each other, this is how we finally die.'

— *Maya Angelou*

'If people thought you were dying, they gave you their full attention.'

— *Chuck Palahniuk*

'If you find it in your heart to care for somebody else, you will have succeeded.'

— *Maya Angelou*

'If you wish to know what a man is, place him in authority.'

— *Yugoslav proverb*

'If someone is going down the wrong road, he doesn't need motivation to speed him up. What he needs is education to turn him around.'

— *Jim Rohn*

'If your happiness depends on what somebody else does, I guess you do have a problem.'

— *Richard Bach*

'If you pick up a starving dog and make him prosperous, he will not bite you. This is the principal difference between a dog and a man.'

— *Mark Twain*

'If the misery of the poor be caused not by the laws of nature, but by our institutions, great is our sin.'

— *Charles Darwin*

'If you don't understand how a woman could both love her sister dearly and want to wring her neck at the same time, then you were probably an only child.'

— *Linda Sunshine*

'If you suspect a man, don't employ him, and if you employ him, don't suspect him.'

— *Chinese proverb*

'If the family were a fruit, it would be an orange, a circle of sections, held together but separable – each segment distinct.'

— *Letty Cottin Pogrebin*

'If you cannot heal the wound, do not tear it open.'

— *Danish proverb*

'If there is beauty in character, there will be harmony in the home. If there is harmony in the home, there will be order in the nation. If there is order in the nation, there will be peace in the world.'

— Confucius

'If you can't forgive and forget, pick one.'

— Robert Brault

'If you dream the proper dreams, and share the myths with people, they will want to grow up to be like you.'

— Ray Bradbury

'If it's very painful for you to criticize your friends – you're safe in doing it. But if you take the slightest pleasure in it, that's the time to hold your tongue.'

— Alice Duer Miller

'If you give what can be taken, you are not really giving. Take what you are given, not what you want to be given. Give what cannot be taken.'

— Idries Shah

'If you were to offer a thirsty man all wisdom, you would not please him more than if you gave him a drink.'

— *Sophocles*

'If you must speak ill of another, do not speak it, write it in the sand near the water's edge.'

— *Napoleon Hill*

'If a friend is in trouble, don't annoy him by asking if there is anything you can do. Think up something appropriate and do it.'

— *Edgar Watson Howe*

'If love does not know how to give and take without restrictions, it is not love, but a transaction that never fails to lay stress on a plus and a minus.'

— *Emma Goldman*

'If you enter this world knowing you are loved and you leave this world knowing the same, then everything that happens in between can be dealt with.'

— *Michael Jackson*

'If we should deal out justice only, in this world, who would escape? No, it is better to be generous, and in the end more profitable, for it gains gratitude for us, and love.'

— *Mark Twain*

'If the mind, that rules the body, ever so far forgets itself as to trample on its slave, the slave is never generous enough to forgive the injury, but will rise and smite the oppressor.'

— *Henry Wadsworth Longfellow*

'If we had no faults of our own, we would not take so much pleasure in noticing those of others.'

— *Francois duc de la Rochefoucald*

'If you were going to die soon and had only one phone call you could make, who would you call and what would you say? And why are you waiting?'

— *Stephen Levine*

'If you haven't any charity in your heart, you have the worst kind of heart trouble.'

— *Bob Hope*

'If my resolution to be a great man was half so strong as it is to despise the shame of being a little one...'

— *William Cowper*

'If those who owe us nothing gave us nothing, how poor we would be.'

— *Antonio Porchia*

'If the world seems cold to you, kindle fires to warm it.'

— *Lucy Larcom*

'If we treated everyone we meet with the same affection we bestow upon our favourite cat, they, too, would purr.'

— *Martin Buxbaum*

'If we don't believe in freedom of expression for people we despise, we don't believe in it at all.'

— *Noam Chomsky*

'If you must love your neighbour as yourself, it is at least as fair to love yourself as your neighbour.'

— *Nicholas de Chamfort*

'If it were not for guests all houses would be graves.'

— *Kahlil Gibran*

'If you are a host to your guest, be a host to his dog also.'

— *Russian proverb*

'If we cannot be clever, we can always be kind.'

— *Alfred Fripp*

'If I love you, what business is it of yours?'

— *Johann Wolfgang von Goethe*

'If you step on people in this life, you're going to come back as a cockroach.'

— *Willie Davis*

'If one remains not annoyed when his greatness is not recognized in his time, isn't he a sage?'

— *Confucius*

'If the human race wishes to have a prolonged and indefinite period of material prosperity, they have only got to behave in a peaceful and helpful way toward one another'

— *Winston Churchill*

'If you look for the bad in people expecting to find it, you surely will.'

— *Abraham Lincoln*

'Ifs...'
foR the AiR foR youR humouR, cReativity and fun

A tip for you so you can 'take flight' in the expansiveness of air to express your humour, creativity and fun...

Oh yes, you can feel the expansiveness of air and space around you, and knowing that you have that space around you, you *can* express your humour, your creativity and your sense of fun.

However, if and when you feel pressured, stressed, worried, concerned, scared or maybe fearful about something, then the air and space around you can feel burdened, heavy, dark perhaps, maybe even contaminated. So, from where you are right now, maybe sitting or resting as you read this, you can begin by discovering if you can feel the expansiveness of 'air' or space around you? You may want to close your eyes or drop your eyes out of focus for a few moments to do this. If you can feel the expansiveness of clean air around you, great.

If you cannot feel expansiveness around you, I do understand, as the spaces around us can become occupied by our emotional or psychological concerns, so here is what you can do: First you need to be at home, or in a room, or place where you can be on your own.

Next, name the space that you are in right now: position

one. Next take three sheets of clean paper, i.e. paper that is not written or drawn or printed on.

Write or draw something on the first sheet to represent your birth. On the second write or draw something to represent your good future, and on the third write or draw something to represent a Happy or Pristine time in your life. If you need time for this, take all the time you need. Then intuitively place these sheets of paper in spaces in the room around you. Take your time. As you do this the spaces around you will begin to make sense.

Next take your time and walk around the room, intuitively sit down if you feel the need, be comfortable as you are comfortably exploring the spaces until you find a clean air expansive space, which may be in or around your happy or pristine space, or an entirely different space.

Next, name this space clean air and know you can return to this space every day: even when you are in a different place, you can still map.

In your clean air expansive space, sit or stand whatever feels right for you, sometimes standing or moving around in the space feels right especially for fun and humour, we have more upbeat energy as we move about.

In your clean air space ask your mind to begin to tune into your creative self. This may seem odd to you at first, so just be curious. When I do this I usually find that my mind is picturing a sky – all kinds of different skies. Then I discover that new and different creative ideas are beginning to incubate. Or fun things. Oh the joy! Or ask your mind to tune in to humour or fun. Just for you.

Elizabeth's Story

If you're being run out of town, get in front of the crowd and make it look like a parade.

— Anonymous

Elizabeth feels stuck, exhausted by what she sees as the chaos in her life. The treasures of her thoughts are dulled by her thoughts that her death is close by.

The fire in her heart is fuelled by her passion for colour and texture in cloth and clothes, which she cannot touch because of the chaos.

Her stability for her bones is in her memorabilia from her history, and her memorabilia is in a clutter of disarray and disorder.

There is very little clean air or space in her world for her creativity.

She courageously makes contact with her clarity to see the permanence of her soul.

Elizabeth, a delightful and elegant lady, during the years of her late sixties and into her early seventies, was grappling with a surfeit of possessions in her home that were a vitally important part of her life and her history; the letters and old family photographs, the furniture, the tapestries and paintings, treasures collected and stored over several decades, precious mementos from her childhood, and possessions accumulated from her different and very successful careers. Elizabeth had been a fashion journalist for a prestigious magazine, next she became a careful and thriving antique dealer, then through her fifties and into her sixties she founded a flourishing healing retreat in the North of England.

It became her time to enjoy her hobbies, particularly her love of clothes. But, to embark upon using and enjoying her amazing collection of textiles and trimmings, the fabrics and delightful silks, the colours and textures, and to create original pieces from her sketches and designs, sleek jackets, elegant shimmering dresses from her fine mixtures of cloths and embroidery, she believed that she needed to first bring order to the chaos she perceived in her memorabilia. Elizabeth feels she needs to make a clear space to be able to create her designs.

She has become stuck in a state of gloom and misery; her skeins of beautiful cloths and vibrant and subtle multi-coloured silk threads remain unopened. She feels totally overwhelmed and fatigued by the enormity of the task confronting her, unable to face her rooms filled with the collected treasures of her life.

But 'If' she brings order to the chaos, 'If' she organises her history, this means to Elizabeth that she will move closer to death.

Every single person on this earth, no matter where they are or what their experiences have been, can discover within their self their own unique brilliance and the genius soul of their creativity.

But Elizabeth's creative soul met the devastating resistance of 'If'.

If she organises her history, which is contained in her belongings and her memorabilia, she will become close to her death. So, she shrinks away into her chaos where she believes she is safe.

Elizabeth's life force is her passion for her creativity; she can colour her world lavishly from a palette of her choice, but 'If' monstrously consumes her passion.

Elizabeth can take flight in the expansiveness of air to express her humour, creativity and fun...

Quotes to continue to take flight in the expansiveness of air to express your humour, creativity and fun...

Air is a fabulous metaphor for considering your humour, creativity and fun, because although we do know that air is composed of oxygen, hydrogen, nitrogen and other gasses, an actual formula is not known. Air does not have a chemical formula because the parts are not chemically combined. So, air for your humour, creativity and fun means those three states or experiences for you can be boundless – not limited by formulae.

'If...' quotes and stories will give you the true feelings of expansiveness when you are worn down, inappropriately grave or solemn, sombre, too staid, too serious, grim, stern, or unsmiling.

'Ifs...' for your humour, creativity and fun will fly you to expansive spaces of mind, restoring you in seconds, or to higher spaces of your limitless potential to happiness, rightful playfulness and moments of frivolity which dissolve those awful tensions, and connect you with your inspirations, ingenuity and inventiveness.

'If someone offers you a gift, and you decline to accept it, the other person still owns that gift. The same is true of insults and verbal attacks.'

— *Steve Pavlina*

'If honour be your clothing, the suit will last a lifetime; but if clothing be your honour, it will soon be worn threadbare.'

— *William Arnot*

'If you have one eye on yesterday, and one eye on tomorrow, you're going to be cockeyed today.'

— *Anonymous*

'If thou canst not see the bottom, wade not.'

— *English proverb*

'If you are in doubt whether to write a letter or not, don't. And the advice applies to many doubts in life besides that of letter writing.'

— *Edward Bulwer Lytton*

'If you can speak three languages you're trilingual. If you can speak two languages you're bilingual. If you can speak only one language you're an American.'

— *Anonymous*

'If you surrender to the wind, you can ride it.'

— *Toni Morrison*

'If a man had as many ideas during the day as he does when he has insomnia, he would make a fortune.'

— *Griff Niblack*

'If a man is proud of his wealth, he should not be praised until it is known how he employs it.'

— *Socrates*

'If you want to make beautiful music, you must play the black and the white notes together.'

— *Richard Nixon*

'If you don't see yourself as a winner, then you cannot perform as a winner.'

— *Zig Ziglar*

'If a child is to keep alive his inborn sense of wonder without any such gift from the fairies, he needs the companionship of at least one adult who can share it, rediscovering with him the joy, excitement, and mystery of the world we live in.'

— *Rachel Carson*

'If you have love you don't need to have anything else. If you don't have, it doesn't matter much what else you do have.'

— *James M. Barrie*

'If the cap fits, wear it.'

— *English proverb*

'If you think it's going to rain, it will.'

— *Clint Eastwood*

'If one has to jump a stream and knows how wide it is, he will not jump. If he does not know how wide it is, he will jump, and six times out of ten he will make it.'

— Persian proverb

'If begging should unfortunately be thy lot, knock at the large gates only.'

— Arabian proverb

'If what you did yesterday seems big, you haven't done anything today.'

— Lou Holtz

'If you want to tell people the truth, make them laugh, otherwise they'll kill you.'

— Oscar Wilde

'If you're not failing every now and again, it's a sign you're not doing anything very innovative.'

— Woody Allen

'If you injure your neighbour, better not do it by halves.'
— *George Bernard Shaw*

'If you are going to walk on thin ice, you might as well dance!'
— *Anonymous*

'If you pretend to be good, the world takes you very seriously. If you pretend to be bad, it doesn't. Such is the astounding stupidity of optimism.'
— *Oscar Wilde*

'If you are not the lead sled dog, the world looks pretty much the same every day.'
— *Anonymous*

'If you don't like how things are, change it! You're not a tree.'
— *Jim Rohn*

'If you're going to be able to look back on something and laugh about it, you might as well laugh about it now.'

— *Marie Osmond*

'If I'd observed all the rules, I'd never have got anywhere.'

— *Marilyn Monroe*

'If you have an hour, will you not improve that hour, instead of idling it away?'

— *Lord Chesterfield*

'If you lose the power to laugh, you lose the power to think.'

— *Clarence Darrow*

'If you're old, don't try to change yourself, change your environment.'

— *B. F. Skinner*

'If you want creative workers, give them enough time to play.'

— *John Cleese*

'If children have the ability to ignore all odds and percentages, then maybe we can all learn from them. When you think about it, what other choice is there but to hope? We have two options, medically and emotionally: give up, or Fight Like Hell.'

— *Lance Armstrong*

'If you were happy every day of your life you wouldn't be a human being, you'd be a game show host.'

— *Gabriel Heatter*

'If a man knew anything, he would sit in a corner and be modest; but he is such an ignorant peacock, that he goes bustling up and down, and hits on extraordinary discoveries.'

— *Ralph Waldo Emerson*

'If you come to a fork in the road, take it.'

— *Yogi Bear*

'If some longing goes unmet, don't be astonished. We call that Life.'

— *Anna Freud*

'If everything seems under control, you're not going fast enough.'

— *Mario Andretti*

'If you think you can, you can. And if you think you can't, you're right.'

— *Mary Kay Ash*

'If you develop an ear for sounds that are musical it is like developing an ego. You begin to refuse sounds that are not musical and that way cut yourself off from a good deal of experience.'

— *John Cage*

'If one is to be called a liar, one may as well make an effort to deserve the name.'

— *A. A. Milne*

'If you wish to forget anything on the spot, make a note that this thing is to be remembered.'

— *Edgar Allan Poe*

'If you can keep your head when all about you are losing theirs, it's just possible you haven't grasped the situation.'

— *Jean Kerr*

'If you know how to spend less than you get, you have the philosopher's stone.'

— *Benjamin Franklin*

'If you are out to describe the truth, leave elegance to the tailor.'

— *Albert Einstein*

'If you wish success in life, make perseverance your bosom friend, experience your wise counsellor, caution your elder brother and hope your guardian genius.'

— *Joseph Addison*

'If you pray for rain, be prepared to deal with some mud.'
— *Mary Englebreit*

'If you wish in this world to advance, your merits you're bound to enhance. You must stir it and stump it, and blow your own trumpet, or trust me, you haven't a chance.'
— *W. S. Gilbert*

'If A is success in life, then A equals x plus y plus z. Work is x; y is play; and z is keeping your mouth shut.'
— *Albert Einstein*

'If you're afraid to let someone else see your weakness, take heart: Nobody's perfect. Besides, your attempts to hide your flaws don't work as well as you think they do.'
— *Julie Morgenstern*

'If I had my life to live over... I'd dare to make more mistakes next time.'
— *Nadine Stair*

'If Jesus Christ were to come today, people would not crucify him. They would ask him to dinner, hear what he had to say, and make fun of it.'

— *Thomas Carlyle*

'If the dead talk to you, you are a spiritualist; if God talks to you, you are a schizophrenic.'

— *Thomas Szasz*

'If God wanted us to be brave, why did He give us legs?'

— *Marvin Kitman*

'If Jesus were here today, he wouldn't be riding around on a donkey. He'd be taking a plane, he'd be using the media.'

— *Joel Osteen*

'If God, as some now say, is dead, He no doubt died of trying to find an equitable solution to the Arab-Jewish problem.'

— *I.F. Stone*

'If you want to catch something, running after it isn't always the best way.'

— *Lois McMaster Bujold (Barrayar)*

'If you want to know what God thinks of money, just look at the people he gave it to.'

— *Dorothy Parker*

'If God had really intended for men to fly, he'd make it easier to get to the airport.'

— *George Winters*

'If it turns out that there is a God, I don't think that he's evil. But the worst that you can say about him is that basically he's an underachiever.'

— *Woody Allen*

'If only God would give me some clear sign! Like making a large deposit in my name in a Swiss bank.'

— *Woody Allen*

'If we were not all so interested in ourselves, life would be so uninteresting that none of us would be able to endure it.'
— *Arthur Schopenhauer*

'If Christ were here now there is one thing he would not be – a Christian.'
— *Mark Twain*

'If God were suddenly condemned to live the life which He has inflicted upon men, He would kill Himself.'
— *Alexander Dumas*

'If more of us valued food and cheer and song above hoarded gold, it would be a merrier world.'
— *J. R. R. Tolkien*

'If in the last few years you haven't discarded a major opinion or acquired a new one, check your pulse. You may be dead.'
— *Gelett Burgess*

'If God would have wanted us to live in a permissive society He would have given us Ten Suggestions and not Ten Commandments.'

— *Zig Zigler*

'If God wants us to do a thing, he should make his wishes sufficiently clear. Sensible people will wait till he has done this before paying much attention to him.'

— *Samuel Butler*

'If I am not allowed to laugh in heaven, I don't want to go there.'

— *Martin Luther*

'If you want to test your memory, try to recall what you were worrying about one year ago today.'

— *E. Joseph Cossman*

'If you wouldn't write it and sign it, don't say it.'

— *Earl Wilson*

'If you smile when no one else is around, you really mean it.'
— *Andy Rooney*

'If you cultivate a healthy poverty and simplicity, so that finding a penny will literally make your day, then, since the world is in fact planted in pennies, you have with your poverty bought a lifetime of days.'
— *Annie Dillard (Pilgrim at Tinker Creek)*

'If you haven't had at least a slight poetic crack in the heart, you have been cheated by nature.'
— *Phyllis Battelle*

'If you can laugh together, you can work together.'
— *Robert Orben*

'If there was less sympathy in the world, there would be less trouble in the world.'
— *Oscar Wilde*

'If you are losing a tug-of-war with a tiger, give him the rope before he gets to your arm. You can always buy a new rope.'
— *Max Gunther*

'If man had created man, he would be ashamed of his performance.'
— *Mark Twain*

'If you would not be forgotten as soon as you are dead and rotten, either write something worth reading or do things worth the writing.'
— *Benjamin Franklin*

'If you obey all the rules you miss all the fun.'
— *Katharine Hepburn*

'If rich people could hire other people to die for them, the poor could make a wonderful living.'
— *Yiddish proverb*

'If you treat every situation as a life and death matter, you'll die a lot of times.'

— Dean Smith

'If we see light at the end of the tunnel, it the light of the oncoming train.'

— Robert Lowell

'If I fall asleep with a pen in my hand, don't remove it – I might be writing in my dreams.'

— Terri Guillemets

'If you die in an elevator, be sure to push the up button.'

— Sam Levenson

'If you hold a cat by the tail you learn things you cannot learn any other way.'

— Mark Twain

'If you would create something, you must be something.'
— *Johann Wolfgang von Goethe*

'If I was dead, I wouldn't know I was dead. That's the only thing I have against death. I want to enjoy my death.'
— *Samuel Beckett*

'If you spend all your time worrying about dying, living isn't going to be much fun.'
— *Roseanne Barr*

'If death meant just leaving the stage long enough to change costume and come back as a new character... Would you slow down? Or speed up?'
— *Chuck Palahniuk*

'If you believe everything you read, better not read.'
— *Japanese proverb*

'If one is lucky, a solitary fantasy can totally transform one million realities.'

— *Maya Angelou*

'If you aren't in over your head, how do you know how tall you are?'

— *T. S. Eliot*

'If we have learned one thing from the history of invention and discovery, it is that, in the long run – and often in the short one – the most daring prophecies seem laughably conservative.'

— *Arthur C. Clarke*

'If you want to make an apple pie from scratch, you must first create the universe.'

— *Carl Sagan*

'If you don't know where you are going, any road will get you there.'

— *Lewis Carroll*

'If it weren't for my lawyer, I'd still be in prison. It went a lot faster with two people digging.'

— *Joe Martin (Mr. Boffo)*

'If you're young enough, any kind of writing you do for a short period of time is a marvellous apprenticeship.'

— *Irwin Shaw*

'If you continually write and read yourself as a fiction, you can change what's crushing you.'

— *Jeannette Winterson*

'If at first you don't succeed, failure may be your style.'

— *Quentin Crisp*

'If in my youth I had realized that the sustaining splendour of beauty of with which I was in love would one day flood back into my heart, there to ignite a flame that would torture me without end, how gladly would I have put out the light in my eyes.'

— *Michelangelo*

'If the world were a logical place, men would ride side saddle.'

— *Rita Mae Brown*

'If I read a book and it makes my whole body so cold no fire can ever warm me, I know that is poetry.'

— *Emily Dickinson*

'If the English language made any sense, a catastrophe would be an apostrophe with fur.'

— *Doug Larson*

'If you can speak what you will never hear, if you can write what you will never read, you have done rare things.'

— *Henry David Thoreau*

'If any man wish to write in a clear style, let him be first clear in his thoughts; and if any would write in a noble style, let him first possess a noble soul.'

— *Johann Wolfgang von Goethe*

'If a writer wrote merely for his time, I would have to break my pen and throw it away.'

— *Victor Hugo*

'If you put tomfoolery into a computer, nothing comes out of it but tomfoolery. But this tomfoolery, having passed through a very expensive machine, is somehow ennobled and no-one dares criticize it.'

— *Pierre Gallois*

'If you think nobody cares if you're alive, try missing a couple of car payments.'

— *Flip Wilson*

'If at first you don't succeed... So much for skydiving.'

— *Henry Youngman*

'If computers get too powerful, we can organize them into a committee – that will do them in.'

— *Bradley's Bromide*

'If you had to identify, in one word, the reason why the human race has not achieved, and never will achieve, its full potential, that word would be 'meetings'.'

— *Dave Barry*

'If you do not breathe through writing, if you do not cry out in writing, or sing in writing, then don't write, because our culture has no use for it.'

— *Anais Nin*

'If I didn't have my films as an outlet for all the different sides of me, I would probably be locked up.'

— *Angelina Jolie*

'If you cannot be a poet, be the poem.'

— *David Carradine*

'If you are possessed by an idea, you find it expressed everywhere, you even *smell* it.'

— *Thomas Mann (Tonio Kröger)*

'If you have the same ideas as everybody else but have them one week earlier than everyone else then you will be hailed as a visionary. But if you have them five years earlier you will be named a lunatic.'

— *Barry Jones*

'If only we could pull out our brain and use only our eyes.'

— *Pablo Picasso*

'If music be the food of love, play on.'

— *William Shakespeare (Twelfth Night)*

'If you have a success you have it for the wrong reasons. If you become popular it is always because of the worst aspects of your work.'

— *Ernest Hemingway*

'If you have the creative urge, it isn't going to go away. But sometimes it takes a while before you accept the fact.'

— *Hugh Macleod*

'If 'ifs' were gifts, every day would be Christmas.'

— Charles Barkley

'If you're yearning for the good old days, just turn off the air conditioning.'

— Griff Niblack

'If you can't read and write you can't think. Your thoughts are dispersed if you don't know how to read and write. You've got to be able to look at your thoughts on paper and discover what a fool you were.'

— Ray Bradbury

'If God had wanted me otherwise, He would have created me otherwise.'

— Johann Wolfgang von Goethe

'If you see the world in black and white, you're missing important grey matter.'

— Jack Fyoch

'If an optimist had his left arm chewed off by an alligator, he might say, in a pleasant and hopeful voice, 'Well, this isn't too bad. I don't have my left arm anymore, but at least nobody will ever ask me whether I am right-handed or left-handed,' but most of us would say something more along the lines of 'Aaaaah! My arm! My arm!''

— *Lemony Snickett*

'If your work speaks for itself, don't interrupt.'

— *Henry J. Kaiser*

'If I were to begin life again, I would devote it to music. It is the only cheap and unpunished rapture upon earth.'

— *Sydney Smith*

'If love is blind, why is lingerie so popular?'

— *Anonymous*

'If you want to kill time, try working it to death.'

— *Sam Levonson*

'If you are a dog and your owner suggests that you wear a sweater...suggest that he wear a tail.'

— *Fran Lebowitz*

'If you can't write your idea on the back of my calling card, you don't have a clear idea.'

— *David Belasco*

'If it keeps up, man will atrophy all his limbs but the push-button finger.'

— *Frank Lloyd Wright*

'If you can solve your problem, then what is the need of worrying? If you cannot solve it, then what is the use of worrying?'

— *Shantideva*

'If you can't get rid of the skeleton in your closet, you'd best teach it to dance.'

— *George Bernard Shaw*

'Ifs...'
for the Diamonds of your Soul

A tip for you so you can know and value the diamond clarity and permanence of your 'soul'...

Maybe soul is not the correct word for you? Maybe your spirit, or your true self, or your true identity or some other word or phrase is for you? A few years ago a wonderful client was looking puzzled as I talked about true identity.

Suddenly he brightened and said: 'Ah, you mean my 'Intended Being''.' My skin tingled with delight, what an exquisitely beautiful description, your Intended Being.

So, you choose the right word or words for you, and forgive me as I continue to use the word soul, which is right for me.

I suggest that you could discover your soul's purpose or intention. I asked this question many years ago, 'What is my soul's purpose?' and the answer for me is: My soul's purpose is to grow itself. And I knew that this was for me the correct answer, because this answer resonated deeply within me. My next question was: 'How do I do that, how do I assist my soul to grow? I have lots of answers, my main answer, or head line answer is: Through compassion. Compassion has clarity for me and a sense of permanence, the value of diamonds.

So, if you are interested: Be somewhere comfortable for you, perhaps your happy or pristine space, close your eyes, or if you prefer drop your eyes out of focus and simply ask: What is my soul's purpose or intention?

This may take a little time but you will begin to get the clarity that you choose to want. If after a few attempts at asking this question perhaps you have no real clarity, then in these quiet moments picture yourself as a child, a contented child. And in your imagination ask the contented child: What is your purpose or intention or what is your soul's purpose or intention?

Once you have clarity on the answer to your soul's purpose or intention, then ask: 'How do I do that?'

And if you do choose to do this I truly wish for you diamond clarity and a sense of permanence.

Tom's Story

If the impulse to daring and bravery is too fierce and violent, stay it with guidance and instruction.

— *Xun Zi*

Tom had been imprisoned in his own home for more than ten years.

His thoughts had been tarnished with the belief that outside his four walls lay madness for him.

He felt so isolated that the fire in his heart had no new, fresh fuel.

He had hardly any inner strength or stability, as his bones shook with terror.

He courageously found spaces with pockets of clean air to express his humour, creativity and fun.

And he felt that the diamond brightness and permanence of his soul had been dulled.

Tom is articulate and thoughtful. His family and numerous friends find it hard to accept that Tom has lived the past ten years and more as a prisoner inside the walls of his own home.

He's tall and lanky, aged forty; he's always got a joke or humorous story to tell. Yet every day he asks: 'If I go outside my house, what will happen next?' He tells himself: 'I feel I will become mad and be a danger to myself...' So everyday he does not leave his home. He cannot risk madness which could lead to his death.

This is his belief, and so he has remained stuck, imprisoned in his own home for more than ten years.

I would safely bet that this man wouldn't harm a fly. He is trapped, caught in his own moral confusion, caught in his own 'If', and so he is quick to imprison himself.

He is attempting to predict, and therefore avoid, the most dreaded future event with his initial 'If'.

How powerful is that? How sad is that?

If he does go outside he's damned with madness and probable death, if he doesn't go outside he's damned to incarceration.

I am sad about his 'If' and I am also glad of it, for it led us to discover the information, unconsciously encoded in his two vital beliefs that he might go mad and be a danger to himself. His beliefs, which are not the truth, have been driving his behaviour for more than ten years.

Better for him to be inside, imprisoned and alive, than outside and dead.

I did not respond to him with, 'Of course you won't go mad!' I asked, 'How do you know you might go mad? And how do you know you might be a danger to yourself?'

His epistemology, that is, how he knows he might go mad, led us on the right journey to untangle, heal and resolve his experiences as a young boy when he had been abandoned.

During this time of abandonment he was in terror, he felt he was going mad, and the only thought that he had, as the way out of his nightmare of madness, was to be dead.

And there we found the younger part of him, in a frozen moment of terror, in the dark, abandoned, overwhelmed with fear.

The young mind will freeze a moment in time, during a

crisis or trauma, in an attempt to protect from the possibility of the next moment becoming worse. The information encoded in that frozen moment will rarely, if ever, change as the years go by; the young part of the mind will rarely, if ever, grow up. As long as he remains frozen in those moments, although he is feeling and believing that he is going mad, he is still alive. In his young mind it is better to be almost mad but still alive, rather than the next moment bringing death.

Tom, aged about twenty-eight, was the victim of a serious and traumatic road accident which caused these unresolved, buried fears from those past frozen moments, to be brought into his conscious awareness of feeling. We could conjecture similarities to his childhood experience such as the accident happening on a dark night on an isolated road, and apart from the vehicle that collided with him as he was on his way home from work on his bicycle, Tom being alone.

We discovered that after his accident Tom started to have horrific visions as he imagined leaving his home, he saw himself screaming and howling in a totally out of control hell which led him to picture throwing himself off a bridge.

Over the years of practicing therapy, I have come to recognise a terrible kind of sadness in some of the people I work with. A vitally important part of them becomes subjugated by what could be called moral depression, because 'If' we behave in a certain way one or more of our morals will be compromised or even destroyed, and 'If' we don't behave in that certain way we experience a constriction and a restriction of a massive part of our true potential.

So what happened to Tom in those moments of his younger life? He unconsciously subjugated his anima.

Carl Gustav Jung identified the anima as the unconscious feminine component of males and the animus as the unconscious masculine component of females. Jungian practitioners believe every person has both anima and animus. Jung stated, 'The anima and animus act as a guide to the unconscious unified self.'

Tom, a boy from a good hard-working family, through his father's, grandfather's and elder brothers' examples, strongly identified with a part of his gender role, that is, boys don't cry. Would Tom's anima have thrived instead of becoming frozen and stuck on that dark night when as a young boy he felt abandoned and lost if he had cried, and cried out for help? Would his anima, instead of being incarcerated for more than ten years, have been able to be on a journey of discovery of his strongly alive passionate soul, to feel purpose, to explore and experience the endless opportunities that abide in the world?

I have been privileged to accompany Tom on a journey to free and heal his younger self from the terror of abandonment, giving him freedom to understand the Ifs along his path and to expand his world.

If when Tom does now choose to go out, he's just going out – nothing bad will happen.

Tom will continue to value the diamonds of his soul's clarity and permanence...

Quotes to continue to value the diamonds of your soul's clarity and permanence...

Soul will mean whatever it does to you, it could mean your true self, the spirit of you, your true identity and so on.

I was truly inspired by the metaphor of diamond coming to me to represent my soul, because diamond symbolises exactly what I believe. You see, the word Diamond comes from the ancient Greek, *adamas*, meaning, *unbreakable*. In all my twenty-seven years of work the soul, no matter the hardship endured by others, the soul of the person is never broken. Two other important qualities of diamonds which I relate to the soul are: they have a very high ability to disperse light - so the light another person shines on our life I would say ultimately will come from the soul. Also, a cut diamond's sparkle is rarely, if ever, contaminated by impurities, so that the soul is the part of us that remains pure no matter the toxins in life.

'If...' quotes and stories will lighten you when you are feeling and thinking hopeless, pessimistic, desperate, discouraged, bleak, impossible, gloomy, cynical thoughts.

'Ifs...' for your soul will restore your hope, and hope will let you know that though from time to time you may feel damaged, you are not breakable, and you do shine light on others.

'If you realize that all things change, there is nothing you will try to hold on to... there is nothing you cannot achieve.'

— *Lao Tzu*

'If a man hasn't discovered something that he will die for, he isn't fit to live.'

— *Martin Luther King, Jr*

'If you have integrity, nothing else matters. If you don't have integrity, nothing else matters.'

— *Alan Simpson*

'If a man has any greatness in him, it comes to light, not in one flamboyant hour, but in the ledger of his daily work.'

— *Beryl Markham*

'If the skies fall, one may hope to catch larks.'

— *Francis Rabelais*

'If your actions inspire others to dream more, learn more, do more and become more, you are a leader.'

— John Quincy Adams

'If you're going to hold someone down you're going to have to hold on by the other end of the chain. You are confined by your own repression.'

— Toni Morrison

'If your efforts are sometimes greeted with indifference, don't lose heart. The sun puts on a wonderful show at daybreak, yet most of the people in the audience go on sleeping.'

— Ada Teixeira

'If our early lessons of acceptance were as successful as our early lessons of anger, how much happier we would all be.'

— Peter McWilliams

'If it is worth taking, it is worth asking for.'

— Gaelic proverb

'If you do not understand a man you cannot crush him. And if you do understand him, very probably you will not.'
— *Gilbert K. Chesterton*

'If you view all the things that happen to you, both good and bad, as opportunities, then you operate out of a higher level of consciousness.'
— *Les Brown*

'If you don't ask, you don't get.'
— *Anonymous*

'If one sticks too rigidly to one's principles, one would hardly see anybody.'
— *Agatha Christie*

'If you haven't found something strange during the day, it hasn't been much of a day.'
— *John A. Wheeler*

'If a man happens to find himself, he has a mansion which he can inhabit with dignity all the days of his life.'

— James A. Michener

'If evil be said of thee, and if it be true, correct thyself; if it be a lie, laugh at it.'

— Epictetus

'If you want things to be different, perhaps the answer is to become different yourself.'

— Norman Vincent Peale

'If opportunity doesn't knock, build a door.'

— Milton Berle

'If we all worked on the assumption that what is accepted as true were really true, there would be little hope of advance.'

— Orville Wright

'If I have learnt anything, it is that life forms no logical patterns. It is haphazard and full of beauties which I try to catch as they fly by, for who knows whether any of them will ever return?'

— *Margot Fonteyn*

'If you enjoy living, it is not difficult to keep the sense of wonder.'

— *Ray Bradbury*

'If you deliberately plan on being less than you are capable of being, then I warn you that you'll be unhappy for the rest of your life.'

— *Abraham Maslow*

'If you pay peanuts, you get monkeys.'

— *English proverb*

'If you put yourself in a position where you have to stretch outside your comfort zone, then you are forced to expand your consciousness.'

— *Les Brown*

'If you follow your bliss, you put yourself on a kind of track, which has been there all the while waiting for you, and the life that you ought to be living is the one you are living.'
— *Joseph Campbell*

'If evil is inevitable, how are the wicked accountable? Nay, why do we call men wicked at all? Evil is inevitable, but is also remediable.'

— *Horace Mann*

'If you want happiness for an hour – take a nap. If you want happiness for a day – go fishing. If you want happiness for a month – get married. If you want happiness for a year – inherit a fortune. If you want happiness for a lifetime – help someone else.'

— *Chinese proverb*

'If you pray for only one thing, .let it be for an idea.'
— *Percy Sutton*

'If you look at life one way, there is always cause for alarm.'
— *Elizabeth Bowen*

'If it is surely the means to the highest end we know, can any work be humble or disgusting? Will it not rather be elevating as a ladder, the means by which we are translated?'

— *Henry David Thoreau*

'If even dying is to be made a social function, then, grant me the favour of sneaking out on tiptoe without disturbing the party.'

— *Dag Hammarskjold*

'If you wouldst live long, live well, for folly and wickedness shorten life.'

— *Benjamin Franklin*

'If we hope for what we are not likely to possess, we act and think in vain, and make life a greater dream and shadow than it really is.'

— *Joseph Addison*

'If humanity does not opt for integrity we are through completely. It is absolutely touch and go. Each one of us could make the difference.'

— *Buckminster Fuller*

'If people are good only because they fear punishment, and hope for reward, then we are a sorry lot indeed.'

— *Albert Einstein*

'If you want to be respected by others the great thing is to respect yourself. Only by that, only by self-respect will you compel others to respect you.'

— *Fyodor Dostoevsky (The Insulted and the Injured)*

'If you can't have faith in what is held up to you for faith, you must find things to believe in yourself, for a life without faith in something is too narrow a space to live.'

— *George E. Woodberry*

'If we resist our passions, it is more because of their weakness than because of our strength.'

— *Francois, duc de la Rochefoucauld*

'If you have done terrible things, you must endure terrible things; for thus the sacred light of injustice shines bright.'

— *Sophocles*

'If thou desire the love of God and man, be humble, for the proud heart, as it loves none but itself, is beloved of none but itself. Humility enforces where neither virtue, nor strength, nor reason can prevail.'

— *Francis Quarles*

'If I take death into my life, acknowledge it, and face it squarely, I will free myself from the anxiety of death and the pettiness of life – and only then will I be free to become myself.'

— *Martin Heidegger*

'If you are lonely when you are alone, you are in bad company.'

— *Jean-Paul Sartre*

'If we had a keen vision of all that is ordinary in human life, it would be like hearing the grass grow or the squirrel's heart beat, and we should die of that roar which is the other side of silence.'

— *George Eliot*

'If you can do what you do best and be happy, you're further along in life than most people.'

— *Leonardo DiCaprio*

'If you're in a bad situation, don't worry it'll change. If you're in a good situation, don't worry it'll change.'

— *John A. Simone, Sr*

'If we shall take the good we find, asking no questions, we shall have heaping measures.'

— *Ralph Waldo Emerson*

'If we are facing in the right direction, all we have to do is keep on walking.'

— *Buddhist saying*

'If I am walking with two other men, each of them will serve as my teacher. I will pick out the good points of the one and imitate them and the bad points of the other and correct them in myself.'

— *Confucius*

'If one dream should fall and break into a thousand pieces, never be afraid to pick one of those pieces up and begin again.'

— *Flavia Weedn*

'If I were Opportunity, I wouldn't just knock, you'd have to sign.'

— *Robert Brault*

'If you have time to whine and complain about something then you have the time to do something about it.'

— *Anthony J. D'Angelo*

'If the mountain won't come to Mohammed, then Mohammed must go to the mountain.'

— *Francis Bacon (Essays)*

'If you doubt yourself, then indeed you stand on shaky ground.'

— *Henrik Ibsen*

'Ifs...'
for the minerals of your bones

A tip for you to be able to digest the minerals and crystals for the strength and stability of your 'bones'...

Our negative, non-constructive thoughts can and do weaken our 'bones'. Working with your thoughts will be assisting the strengthening of your bones. Excellent!

We generally tend to believe that for the bones of us to be, and to feel strong and stable that we need security. We need to feel the secure foundations of the minerals and crystals of the earth our home. What our bones really need is for us to feel strong and secure within our self, our inner home, no matter what is happening in the emotional weather outside of us. So, here are two tips for your inner strength and stability of your bones.

Take just a few moments each day to be quiet and comfortable. Close your eyes, or if it feels more comfortable just let your eyes be out of focus like a day dream state, and request that your mind take you to a time that was pristine.

By pristine I mean a time when the external weather was at one with you, and you felt at one with your internal weather — you felt at home inside and out. Request that your mind take you back, if you can, to a time before the cracks came along, no matter how small the cracks may have been, or before you felt tainted or tarnished. If you can get to a pristine time, then stay with it, allow yourself to absorb or digest deep within you the sense of the real security and stability of that time. Keep going back to that time, nourish your bones and you will bring the strengths of the Pristine time into your present reality.

If you cannot discover a Pristine time, here is another tip for you to bring that inner strength and stability. You will need to stand up for this one, if you cannot physically stand up then simply imagine, make pictures of yourself standing up. Stand with your feet facing forward and hip width apart. Take a few moments to get the balance of your body right, head up, shoulders relaxed, arms relaxed by your side. Consider this stance to be your state of inner balance. Intuit which side of your body will want to represent your ability to say 'No', your ability to go forward into the world, and which side of your body will want to represent your ability to say 'Yes', and to step back from the world. Whether you are male or female, consider that your 'No' comes from your masculine self, and your 'Yes' comes from your feminine self. And that for most of us we do have a lack of continued harmony and balance between our inner masculine and feminine self.

Feel your balance; take your time from where you stand. Next shift your balance to 'Yes' side and foot, and then take just one step with your 'No' foot and side forward and state out loud, 'No!' or 'You are wrong' – or 'That is wrong'... and so on, anything that you will know is wanting to be expressed from your masculine self. Practice your tone of voice. You are not yelling you are creating a firm and congruent tone of voice. Feel the energy of your voice. Feel the energy flow inside your body, feel the energy in your bones.

Then move your 'No' side back to your balanced state. Take a moment to feel your balance. Take your 'Yes' side and move your 'Yes' foot and side one step back, keeping your 'No' foot where it was. As you take your step back say out loud 'Yes!' – or 'You are right' – or 'That is right' and anything else that you feel your feminine self wants or needs to express. Create a tone with your voice that is firm, not a door mat tone of voice. Feel the energy of your 'Yes' voice, feel the energy flow inside you. Oddly you will feel the strength of your 'Yes' voice strengthening your bones. Keep practicing... Enjoy!

Jonny's Story

If it is not right do not do it; if it is not true do not say it.

— *Marcus Aurelius*

Jonny had been suffering migraine every day for several months, unable to leave his bed.

His thoughts and beliefs that he could never say the word 'No' had dulled and diminished him the perceived pressure from others had caused him too much pain.

In his heart he felt that to say the word 'No' would cause unhappiness and turmoil in others.

His bones needed him to say 'No' to give him inner stability and inner balance.

He felt that the pressure from others totally filled the space around him, and there was no air available for humour or creativity and fun...

And he felt that the diamond brightness and permanence of his soul had been split in half.

A young man in his early thirties, Jonny had been suffering migraine every day for many months. He had a voice that sounded very young and was barely above a whisper.

We discovered that as a small child he always wanted to be kind to others and to take care of them; he felt totally responsible for those around him to make their lives comfortable and easy. Through those early years of life he learned he could never say 'No'; the expression of this word, in his perception, would cause stormy confusion and discomfort in others.

Jonny's mother had been disabled before Jonny was born. She was clearly a good woman, but when Jonny was a small boy her own understandable unhappiness and frustration manifested in storms of dissatisfaction whenever Jonny said 'No'.

Finally in his early thirties, without an inner ability to say 'No', the unintentional pressure from colleagues and friends reached catastrophe, and his unconscious found a way out. Migraine.

As long as he was lying in bed day after day with migraine, there was no pressure from others.

If he stays in bed he is damned – with migraine.

If he doesn't have the migraine he will have to leave his bed, and then he is damned – with the pressure from others.

Jonny's medication subdued the pain, but not enough for him to get out of bed, and actually nothing was really resolved, as emotionally and psychologically Jonny was still diminished.

As Jonny and I started our work together to resolve his migraines his fear surfaced. He said, 'If I stop having migraines I will have to go out in the world again and experience the pressures from others.'

When we are working intently to resolve a problem we will always be having important dreams, as the amazing paradox is that although a symptom manifests from the unconscious – that is, we of course do not *consciously* want the symptom – the unconscious is actually working to resolve the problem. Our dreams amazingly give us pure unconscious, important information towards solutions and resolutions.

Jonny told me that in his dream he was about to enter a

space that he knew was wrong for him; he felt a kind of danger. He knew that the right thing was to say to his companions, 'No, I am not going there!' In his dream he ignored what he knew, he went along with his companions, and upon entering the space he was suddenly under attack. The wisdom of Jonny's dream had opened the door to him knowing his truth of when to say 'No', in difficult situations. My question: 'And when you know that a space is wrong for you and you need to say 'No', to entering that space, how do you know that you need to say 'No'?'

Jonny answered: 'I know because I have a feeling, like a signal in my stomach.' And herein lay the information needed to cure his problem. The signal in his stomach wanted him to say 'No'.

The catastrophe, the last straw on the camel's back, the final additional small burden that made the entirety of Jonny's difficulties unbearable, happened a few months before he came to me, and manifested as migraines; pain in his head.

As the philosopher and mathematician, Immanuel Kant stated; entirely correctly, 'The symptom is the solution; it is searching for the problem.'

Jonny's problem was that he had learnt as a small boy to ignore the signal in his stomach. This discovery was an epiphanic moment for Jonny.

Jonny was learning to respond to the signal in his stomach; the quality and tone of his voice was beginning to change when Jonny had another 'If'.

You might have guessed it.

His 'If' predicted that, if he said 'No', people in his world would be unhappy and he could not carry the burden of this responsibility.

Jonny did learn to respond to the signal in his stomach,

and learnt to say 'No' in a way that is right and appropriate for him and for his life as he chooses. He did learn that he can say 'No' and also be a kind and caring person, and he discovered that others can take responsibility for their own happiness. He can now say 'No', when he feels pressured and therefore there is no purpose for migraines, which, I am very glad to say, are now resolved.

Jonny will continue to digest the minerals and crystals for strength and stability of his bones...

Laura's Story

If we survive danger it steels our courage more than anything else.

— *Reinhold Niebuhr*

If people can be educated to see the lowly side of their own natures, it may be hoped that they will also learn to understand and to love their fellow men better. A little less hypocrisy and a little more tolerance towards oneself can only have good results in respect for our neighbour; for we are all too prone to transfer to our fellows the injustice and violence we inflict upon our own natures.

— *Carl Jung*

Laura is a young Irish woman. It was a leap of faith for her to meet me and for her to consider what I do, and for her to contemplate working with me.

Laura now speaks to you in the first person – this is Laura's voice of truth:

'I was a radio presenter when I first met Sally. A necessity of a profession in radio is an over-verbal life, meaning of course that words are constantly important.

The absolute simplicity of Sally's four words 'I can help you' so connected with me. These words made more sense than a million sentences, because inside I was able to make some truly important connection and say 'Yes, I do need help'. Until that moment I had been unable to admit this. It was like my 'soul' answered with the simple, 'Yes, I need help.'

I felt frightened as I thought 'If' I start on this journey to heal, I have a fear that it would not happen, it could not happen and that no-one could help me.

You see, I had learnt to live with a wounded soul and I was so afraid to have any expectation for myself to heal in case I could never be healed.

I once heard someone say something like, 'If you've got to know the devil, it's better than a god you may never know.' These words kind of made sense as I'd made the 'devil', or maybe more accurately what 'bedevilled' me, work for me, or so I believed.

I thought: 'What 'If' I am not strong enough to help myself?'

This was definitely a fear for me as I had managed my pain and I had used my pain as something positive by helping others, and being successful.

I wore wigs, they were big and really quite outrageous, they obscured my face all the time. I hid in my wigs, I also hid in my outrageousness; I hid in my big personality.

I hid my pain.

The idea of curing my alopecia and taking off the wig was huge. There were two major things for me: the curing of alopecia was inconceivable, then to take off the wigs. I thought I would be inconsolable because wigs had become a safe place to hide but I did deep down know that safe places to hide can and do become prisons for the soul.

I now realise that, as my work progressed with Sally, I came away from radio because I was in radio in prove a point, and the point was I couldn't be beaten.

But I had been.

I had taken beatings in my life, but I refused, totally

refused, to 'lie down' and let them take me. I had to hold on to who I was inside, I had to jump back up and jump back onto my feet like I was stronger and more outrageous than anyone else. Stronger than where the beatings came from.

Because, when I was beaten I was silenced and I had no voice, and the reason that I wanted to be in radio so much was to have a voice and be heard. When I was beaten it was obviously a huge secret and in those moments my ambition was to be the opposite of silence, to be on radio to have a voice that could and would tell the truth.

One day I would break the silence and use it to help others. I knew one day my story would be told, I knew one day my story would help others. It was why during those times of horror I so adamantly held onto myself. Speaking this now I feel like I have come full circle, this is my day.

Through my work, my journey with Sally I was afraid that my hair would not grow back and 'If' it did it would not be enough.

'If' I took off all my armour *I* would not be enough.

I was also truly afraid that 'If' I then grew through this healing journey I would not be good enough.

Before I met Sally I shaved off all my hair. This meant that I took control, I took control of the alopecia, I took control over wigs, and I took control over myself.

I made this my identity and I took charge, I cut my hair off down to the wick, I dictated which wig to wear.

By working with Sally and handing over to Sally my soul and my heart, I believed that I was handing over the control, I was moving away from a false consciousness I was opening myself up to something I did not necessarily know what the outcome would be and therefore not be able to control.

When I was handing Sally my wounded soul which I had learnt to keep and to live with, this did feel like a massive step, to give all this up I thought I would lose my 'say'.

One day during three or four intensive days of my work with Sally, she told me about a dream that she had the night before.

Sally had also suffered alopecia about eight years before I met her, and she had resolved this problem with her work, and had also done this work with a number of others, helping them to resolve their hair loss.

Sally, I believe has an inherent desire to assist to heal those who are suffering and you can believe me, those who have alopecia, as I did, are really suffering.

Sally said that in her dream she was writing a course that would help many, many sufferers to heal alopecia, and she woke up singing. She was singing out loud, happily, joyously, Stevie Nicks and Fleetwood Mac 'You Can Go Your Own Way.'

But Sally was actually singing: 'You can *grow* your own way!'

She and I enthusiastically found the song and sang together boisterously: 'You can *grow* your own way!'

The song became like a vitally important signature, something distinctive for me, something that identifies *me*.

The song made me realise that Sally never had control of my journey; she was and is a gifted guide and assistant, she enabled me to find my own way.

When I was packing my desk to leave the radio station and my job, I was wondering what would be the last song to be played on the station for me to walk away to, and into a new life.

Yeah, you got it, on came Stevie Nicks, Fleetwood Mac: 'You Can Go Your Own Way!'

And so I did – and so I do...

I Grow My Own Way...
I Go My Own Way...

My need for control had come from an inner place that was not pure, it was not organic; it came from a contrived place within to hide my pain and wounds.

Think of a wig; it is not organic.

This new control that I now have comes from a place of thoughts and words that are just me, and are organic and have the infinite potential for being pure and true.

My hair? I grow my own hair.

It is lush, it has grown and flourishes...

And so do I...'

Laura will continue to bring stability of minerals to her bones...

To continue to digest the minerals for strength and stability of your bones...

'If...' quotes and stories for your bones will assist you in seconds to 'take the correct step' in life when you are feeling indecisive, stuck, wavering, vacillating, when you feel:

> *If, you take the road on the right you'll have nothing left, and if you take the road on the left you'll have nothing right.*
> — *Mark Wright (age eighteen)*

'Ifs...' for your bones will help you 'crystallise' your resolve, sureness and determination to take a correct 'step', and more deeply and life-changing, a correct path for your life.

> *Size aside, there are very few differences between the crystals impregnating your bones and a rock made of hydroxyapatite crystal you find lying on the ground...*
> — *Dr Marc McKee*

'If knowledge and foresight are too penetrating and deep, unify them with ease and sincerity.'

— *Xun Zi*

'If it fails, admit it frankly and try another. But above all, try something.'

— *Franklin D. Roosevelt*

'If we could first know where we are, and whither we are tending, we could then better judge what to do, and how to do it.'

— *Abraham Lincoln*

'If you can't hear the angels, try quieting the static of worry.'

— *Terri Guillemets*

'If you are losing your leisure, look out; you may be losing your soul.'

— *Logan P. Smith*

'If you hear a voice within you say 'you cannot paint,' then by all means paint, and that voice will be silenced.'

— Vincent Van Gogh

'If you always put limit on everything you do, physical or anything else. It will spread into your work and into your life. There are no limits. There are only plateaus, and you must not stay there, you must go beyond them.'

— Bruce Lee

'If we wait for the moment when everything, absolutely everything is ready, we shall never begin.'

— Ivan Turgenev

'If people do not believe that mathematics is simple, it is only because they do not realize how complicated life is.'

— John Louis von Neumann

'If a job is worth doing it is worth doing well.'

— English proverb

'If you learn from defeat, you haven't really lost.'

— *Zig Ziglar*

'If what you are doing is not moving you towards your goals, then it's moving you away from your goals.'

— *Brian Tracy*

'If you once forfeit the confidence of your fellow citizens, you can never regain their respect and esteem. You may fool all of the people some of the time; you can even fool some of the people all the time; but you can't fool all of the people all of the time.'

— *Abraham Lincoln*

'If you want to sing out, sing out, and if you want to be free, be free.'

— *Cat Stevens*

'If you love life, don't waste time, for time is what life is made up of.'

— *Bruce Lee*

'If you want milk, don't sit on a stool in the middle of a field in the hope that the cow will back up to you.'

— English saying

'If you are carrying strong feelings about something that happened in your past, they may hinder your ability to live in the present.'

— Les Brown

'If you stop every time a dog barks, your road will never end.'

— Arabian proverb

'If they give you ruled paper, write the other way.'

— Juan Ramon Jiminez

'If you haven't all the things you want, be grateful for the things you don't have that you wouldn't want.'

— Anonymous

'If you would hit the mark, you must aim a little above it; Every arrow that flies feels the attraction of earth.'
                                    — *Henry Wadsworth Longfellow*

'If I don't practice the way I should, then I won't play the way that I know I can.'
                                    — *Ivan Lendl*

'If you train hard, you'll not only be hard, you'll be hard to beat.'
                                    — *Herschel Walker*

'If you worried about falling off the bike, you'd never get on.'
                                    — *Lance Armstrong*

'If I were asked to give what I consider the single most useful bit of advice for all humanity it would be this: Expect trouble as an inevitable part of life and when it comes, hold you head high, look it squarely in eye and say, 'I will be bigger than you. You cannot defeat me'.'
                                    — *Ann Landers*

'If you keep your mouth shut you will never put your foot in it.'

— *Austin O'Malley*

'If you forget you have to struggle for improvement you go backward.'

— *Geoffrey Hickson*

'If you see a whole thing – it seems that it's always beautiful. Planets, lives... But close up a world's all dirt and rocks. And day to day, life's a hard job, you get tired, you lose the pattern.'

— *Ursula K. Le Guin*

'If you will call your troubles experiences, and remember that every experience develops some latent force within you, you will grow vigorous and happy, however adverse your circumstances may seem to be.'

— *John Heywood*

'If you can't get to be uncommon through going straight, you'll never get to do it through going crooked.'

— *Charles Dickens (Great Expectations)*

'If you scatter thorns, don't go barefoot.'

— *Italian proverb*

'If you can find a path with no obstacles, it probably doesn't lead anywhere.'

— *Frank A. Clark*

'If the wind will not serve, take to the oars.'

— *Latin proverb*

'If you aspire to the highest place, it is no disgrace to stop at the second, or even the third, place.'

— *Cicero*

'If I had a formula for bypassing trouble, I would not pass it around. Trouble creates a capacity to handle it. I don't embrace trouble; that's as bad as treating it as an enemy. But I do say: meet it as a friend, for you'll see a lot of it, and had better be on speaking terms with it.'

— *Oliver Wendell Holmes*

'If your determination is fixed, I do not counsel you to despair. Few things are impossible to diligence and skill. Great works are performed not by strength, but perseverance.'

— *Samuel Johnson*

'If we must fall, we should boldly meet the danger.'

— *Publius Cornelius Tacticus*

'If ever there was a cause, if ever there can be a cause, worthy to be upheld by all of toil or sacrifice that the human heart can endure, it is the cause of Education.'

— *Horace Mann*

'If you greatly desire something, have the guts to stake everything on obtaining it.'

— *Brendan Francis*

'If I take care of my character, my reputation will take care of me.'

— *Dwight L. Moody*

'If you live among wolves you have to act like a wolf.'
— *Nikita Khrushchev*

'If it's what you do and you can do it, then you do it.'
— *Van Morrison*

'If your work is becoming uninteresting, so are you. Work is an inanimate thing and can be made lively and interesting only by injecting yourself into it. Your job is only as big as you are.'
— *George C. Hubbs*

'If you treat people right they will treat you right…ninety percent of the time.'
—*Franklin D. Roosevelt*

'If you limit your choices only to what seems possible or reasonable, you disconnect yourself from what you truly want, and all that is left is a compromise.'
— *Robert Fritz*

'If a man does not keep pace with his companions, perhaps it is because he hears a different drummer. Let him step to the music which he hears, however measured or far away.'

— *Henry David Thoreau*

'If you woke up breathing, congratulations! You have another chance.'

— *Andrea Boydston*

'If you are living out of a sense of obligation you are slave.'

— *Wayne Dyer*

'If your lens is prejudice, you're wearing the wrong prescription.'

— *Carrie Latet*

'If I am not pleased with myself, but should wish to be other than I am, why should I think highly of the influences which have made me what I am?'

— *John Lancaster Spalding*

'If you think you're free, there's no escape possible.'
— *Ram Dass*

'If someone loves a flower of which just one example exists among all the millions and millions of stars, that's enough to make him happy when he looks at the stars.'
— *Antoine de Saint-Exupery*

'If you search the world for happiness, you may find it in the end, for the world is round and will lead you back to your door.'
— *Robert Brault*

'If most of us are ashamed of shabby clothes and shoddy furniture, let us be more ashamed of shabby ideas and shoddy philosophies... It would be a sad situation if the wrapper were better than the meat wrapped inside it.'
— *Albert Einstein*

'If you are neutral in situations of injustice, you have chosen the side of the oppressor. If an elephant has its foot on the tail of a mouse and you say that you are neutral, the mouse will not appreciate your neutrality.'
— *Bishop Desmond Tutu*

'If it takes a lot of words to say what you have in mind, give it more thought.'

— *Dennis Roth*

'If falsehood, like truth, had but one face, we would be more on equal terms. For we would consider the contrary of what the liar said to be certain. But the opposite of truth has a hundred thousand faces and an infinite field.'

— *Michel Eyquem de Montaigne*

'If the past cannot teach the present and the father cannot teach the son, then history need not have bothered to go on, and the world has wasted a great deal of time.'

— *Russell Hoban*

'If malice or envy were tangible and had a shape, it would be the shape of a boomerang.'

— *Charley Reese*

'If you must be in a hurry, then let it be according to the old adage, and hasten slowly.'

— *Saint Vincent de Paul*

'If you observe a really happy man you will find him building a boat, writing a symphony, educating his son, growing double dahlias in his garden, or looking for dinosaur eggs in the Gobi desert. He will not be searching for happiness as if it were a collar button that has rolled under the radiator. He will not be striving for it as a goal in itself. He will have become aware that he is happy in the course of living life twenty-four crowded hours of the day.'
— *W. Beran Wolfe*

'If men were angels, no government would be necessary.'
— *James Madison*

'If you want to look like the people next door, you're probably smothering yourself and your dreams.'
— *Clive Barker*

'If one truly has lost hope, one would not be on hand to say so.'
— *Eric Bentley*

'If at first, the idea is not absurd, then there is no hope for it.'
— *Albert Einstein*

'If we are ever in doubt about what to do, it is a good rule to ask ourselves what we shall wish on the morrow that we had done.'

— *John Lubbock*

'If you believe the doctors, nothing is wholesome; if you believe the theologians, nothing is innocent; if you believe the military, nothing is safe.'

— *Lord Salisbury*

'If we open a quarrel between past and present, we shall find that we have lost the future.'

— *Winston Churchill*

'If moral behaviour were simply following rules, we could program a computer to be moral.'

— *Samuel P. Ginder*

'If you pour oil and vinegar into the same vessel, you would call them not friends but opponents.'

— *Aeschylus*

'If our house be on fire, without inquiring whether it was fired from within or without, we must try to extinguish it.'
— *Thomas Jefferson*

'If I were to wish for anything, I should not wish for wealth and power, but for the passionate sense of the potential, for the eye which, ever young and ardent, sees the possible. Pleasure disappoints possibility never. And what wine is so sparkling, what so fragrant, what so intoxicating, as possibility!'
— *Soren Kierkegaard*

'If fame is only to come after death, I am in no hurry for it.'
— *Marcus Valerius Martial*

'If we had no winter, the spring would not be so pleasant: if we did not sometimes taste of adversity, prosperity would not be so welcome.'
— *Anne Bradstreet*

'If you do not wish to be prone to anger, do not feed the habit; give it nothing which may tend to its increase.'
— *Epictetus*

'If the laws could speak for themselves, they would complain of the lawyers.'

— *George Savile*

'If only closed minds came with closed mouths.'

— *Anonymous*

'If the only new thing we have to offer is an improved version of the past, then today can only be inferior to yesterday. Hypnotized by images of the past, we risk losing all capacity for creative change.'

— *Robert Hewison*

'If we were all to be judged by our thoughts, the hills would be swarming with outlaws.'

— *Johann Sigurjonsson*

'If you have an apple and I have an apple and we exchange these apples then you and I will still each have one apple. But if you have an idea and I have an idea and we exchange these ideas, then each of us will have two ideas.'

— *George Bernard Shaw*

'If you want to know your true opinion of someone, watch the effect produced in you by the first sight of a letter from him.'

— *Arthur Schopenhauer*

'If at first you don't succeed, try, try again. Then quit. There's no use being a damn fool about it.'

— *W. C. Fields*

'If you have a talent, use it in every which way possible. Don't hoard it. Don't dole it out like a miser. Spend it lavishly like a millionaire intent on going broke.'

— *Brendan Francis*

'If your ship doesn't come in, swim out to it!'

— *Jonathan Winters*

'If a window of opportunity appears, don't pull down the shade.'

— *Thomas J. Peters*

'If you believe in what you are doing, then let nothing hold you up in your work. Much of the best work of the world has been done against seeming impossibilities. The thing is to get the work done.'

— *Dale Carnegie*

'If I set for myself a task, be it so trifling, I shall see it through. How else shall I have confidence in myself to do important things?'

— *George Clason*

'If you're not brave, you're not going to be free.'

— *Newt Gingrich*

'If necessity is the mother of invention, discontent is the father of progress.'

— *David Rockefeller*

'If you ever need a helping hand, you'll find one at the end of your arm.'

— *Yiddish proverb*

'If fate means you to lose, give him a good fight anyhow.'
— *William McFee*

'If one begins all deeds well, it is likely that they will end well too.'
— *Sophocles*

'If they can make penicillin out of mouldy bread, they can sure make something out of you.'
— *Muhammad Ali*

'If ever there is tomorrow when we're not together...there is something you must always remember. You are braver than you believe, stronger than you seem, and smarter than you think. But the most important thing is, even if we're apart...I'll always be with you.'
— *A. A. Milne (Winnie the Pooh)*

'If you hide your ignorance, no one will hit you, and you'll never learn.'
— *Ray Bradbury (Fahrenheit 451)*

'If you worry about what might be, and wonder what might have been, you will ignore what is.'

— *Anonymous*

'If you're still hanging onto a dead dream of yesterday, laying flowers on its grave by the hour, you cannot be planting the seeds for a new dream to grow today.'

— *Joyce Chapman*

'If a man harbours any sort of fear, it percolates through all thinking, damages his personality and makes him a landlord to a ghost.'

— *Lloyd Douglas*

'If you want to make your dreams come true, the first thing you have to do is wake up.'

— *J. M. Power*

'If we make a couple of discoveries here and there we need not believe things will go on like this for ever. Just as we hit water when we dig in the earth, so we discover the incomprehensible sooner or later.'

— *Georg C. Lichtenberg*

'If you cannot do great things, do small things in a great way.'

— Napoleon Hill

'If you have competence, you pretty much know its boundaries already. To ask the question (of whether you are past the boundary) is to answer it.'

— Charlie Munger

'If you get up one more time than you fall you will make it through.'

— Chinese proverb

'If we say it long enough eventually we're going to reap a harvest. We're going to get exactly what we're saying.'

— Joel Osteen

'If you feel you are down on your luck, check the level of your effort.'

— Robert Brault

'If you don't want to do something, one excuse is as good as another.'

— Yiddish proverb

'If experience was so important, we'd never have had anyone walk on the moon.'

— Doug Rader

'If one does not know to which port one is sailing, no wind is favourable.'

— Seneca

'If the shoe fits, you're not allowing for growth.'

— Robert N. Coons

'If I had to live my life again, I'd make the same mistakes, only sooner.'

— Tallulah Bankhead

'If people only knew how hard I work to gain my mastery, it wouldn't seem so wonderful at all.'
                                        — *Michelangelo Buonarroti*

'If I have ever made any valuable discoveries, it has been owing more to patient attention, than to any other talent.'
                                        — *Isaac Newton*

'If I despised myself, it would be no compensation if everyone saluted me, and if I respect myself, it does not trouble me if others hold me lightly.'
                                        — *Max Nordau*

'If I had my life to live over, I would perhaps have more actual troubles but I'd have fewer imaginary ones.'
                                        — *Don Herold*

'If things go wrong, don't go with them.'
                                        — *Roger Babson*

'If to do were as easy as to know what were good to do, chapels had been churches, and poor men's cottages princes' palaces.'

— *William Shakespeare*

'If we do not plant knowledge when young, it will give us no shade when we are old.'

— *Lord Chesterfield*

'If you can't do what you want, do what you can.'

— *Lois McMaster Bujold (Memory)*

'If we attend continually and promptly to the little that we can do, we shall ere long be surprised to find how little remains that we cannot do.'

— *Samuel Butler*

'If your success is not on your own terms, if it looks good to the world but does not feel good in your heart, it is not success at all.'

— *Anna Quindlen*

'If we all did the things we are capable of doing, we would literally astound ourselves.'

— *Thomas Edison*

'If you really want to do something, you do it. You don't save it for a sound bite.'

Liz Friedman (House M.D.)

'If man makes himself a worm he must not complain when he is trodden on.'

— *Immanuel Kant*

'If you don't make mistakes, you're not working on hard enough problems. And that's a big mistake.'

— *Frank Wilczek*

'If you want to lift yourself up, lift up someone else.'

— *Booker T. Washington*

'If it were not for hopes, the heart would break.'

— *Thomas Fuller*

'If human beings are perceived as potentials rather than problems, as possessing strengths instead of weaknesses, as unlimited rather that dull and unresponsive, then they thrive and grow to their capabilities.'

— *Robert Conklin*

'If we could all hear one another's prayers, God might be relieved of some of his burdens.'

— *Ashleigh Brilliant*

'If a mistake is not a stepping stone, it is a mistake.'

— *Eli Siegel*

'If you have the will to win, you have achieved half your success; if you don't, you have achieved half your failure.'

— *David Ambrose*

'If you don't get everything you want, think of the things you don't get that you don't want.'

— *Oscar Wilde*

'If you would attain to what you are not yet, you must always be displeased by what you are. For where you are pleased with yourself there you have remained. Keep adding, keep walking, keep advancing.'

— *Saint Augustine*

'If you're trying to achieve, there will be roadblocks. I've had them; everybody has had them. But obstacles don't have to stop you. If you run into a wall, don't turn around and give up. Figure out how to climb it, go through it, or work around it.'

— *Michael Jordan*

'If you wait, all that happens is that you get older.'

— *Larry McMurtry*

'Ifs...'

for the 'Gold' of your thoughts

If you are going to build something in the air it is always better to build castles than houses of cards.

— *Georg C. Lichtenberg*

A tip to bring the purity of gold to your thoughts...

We cannot simply make a decision to have only positive 'pure gold' thoughts and 'hey presto' negative thoughts just vanish! This strategy does not work, though it may appear to work for a while. When positive thinking works for a while, it's because we have plastered over the cracks, and our life looks good, until the cracks inevitably reappear. All of us, pretty much, for any and every reason you can conceive of, have been tarnished with destructive – to ourselves and to others – thoughts and believes.

So, here is something that we can do to mend the cracks, cleanse off the dust and reveal the gold. Notice your thoughts, learn to observe and take note of them. And 'If' your thoughts are not constructive, and are not supportive of your life and celebrating your life, then begin to change them. How do we do this? We used to believe that our thoughts are 'hard wired', and we cannot change them. This is not the truth.

So, what you can do first of all as you take note of negative or destructive thoughts, is make categories. What do I mean by this? Here is a really good example: a client came to me and said that he had lots and lots of negative thoughts, which he called 'worries'. I asked him: 'About how many worries do you have?' He answered: 'Oh, hundreds and hundreds...' As I asked him to name them, we discovered that he had seven categories. Here are some examples of his categories:

His concerns about his health.

His fears about his job.

His unease about his son's future.

Once we have the categories organised we can then begin to work on each one at a time to discover solutions, rather than being too overwhelmed or feeling too fraught to move on.

Take each of your categories, one at a time, (you may discover that you only have one!) then ask your dreams to give you solutions. Dreams of course give us important unconscious information; our unconscious is continually working towards our health and well being.

Let's take my lovely client, a man conscientious about his family and his job; he first came to work with me because he could not swallow food, which is why he was particularly concerned about his health. Each night as he was dropping off to sleep my client would ask, taking one category at a time: 'I want my dreams to give me important information towards solutions for my health; my dreams will be comfortable dreams.'

If you choose to work with this tip, soon you will gain amazing insights and solutions from your dreams, solutions that you literally had never thought of before. And sometimes, just sometimes, there are no solutions as such and the solution is to just 'walk away', let it go, do something entirely different.

So as you are dropping off to sleep say, silently but with 'strength' of feeling in your inner 'voice', like you mean it: 'I want my dreams to give me solutions to 'X', (that is, state the title of your group of thoughts)' and always add: 'My dreams *will* be comfortable dreams.'

Soon you will begin to receive solutions from your dreams. You may not remember the dreams, but you'll notice changes in your thoughts and behaviour in a positive way.

Next you may notice some habitual thoughts continuing. Noticing and observing does begin to make huge changes to these thought patterns.

And, for some that may persist, play with them!

What do I mean? Well, for example you can change the letters of the words around, jumble them up, and make nonsense of them. Once you've made nonsense of them you play the nonsense in your mind, or out loud. Play with the nonsense, set it to music! Would an example help? OK – try this simple one; a thought (about yourself) like: 'You're stupid!' could become: 'Eruoy diputs!' Saying this out loud and laughing because you cannot help laughing at the 'stupidity' of such a thought, works really, really fast. You'll notice that soon you will never hear, the 'You're stupid!' in your thoughts again... Enjoy!

You can have such creative fun with patterns of negative thoughts. Here is one of mine; I hope it makes you smile. Many years ago when I was working with my therapists, the amazing David Grove, and the wondrous Dr Rossi, I noticed a habitual thought of mine. When I was little there was not much money and my mother could not afford for me to be clumsy, so if I dropped a cup or spilled my food she would say to me, crisply annoyed, 'For goodness sake...' and my stomach would clench uncomfortably. Then during the time of my therapy work one day at home I dropped a cup and as I felt my stomach clench in pain I heard in my habitual thought: 'For goodness sake...' I immediately started dancing around the kitchen singing very loudly, entirely out of tune, '... for goodness sake... do the hippy, hippy shake...'

After only two more spilling or dropping occasions and singing and dancing, I have never had that thought again – and I decided to ask myself to learn to be more careful. I realised that I was actually quite clumsy because I was always rushing, as I'd always felt I didn't have enough time, so I also learnt from this one 'negative' thought to have a much more harmonious relationship with time. Now that is a big one – that is gold.

I really am not disrespecting you, as I do know that some of your negative thoughts will have serious or important content for you, and for others. Discover the serious gold by paying attention to the thought, writing the thought down, and beginning a focused process of cleaning away the 'dust' or 'grit' or 'muck' to create pure, valuable, gold thoughts for yourself.

Annie's Story

If I believe I will achieve.

— *Libby Bolton*

Annie had been suffering complex symptoms for many years.

The bright gold of her thoughts had been cloaked and buried beneath dark, heavy fears.

The fire in her heart had almost died, yet Annie had the great courage to keep discovering some fuel to keep the fading embers alight.

Her bones felt almost totally without substance.

She 'flew high' with great effort to find clean air for her good humour and creativity.

And we found that she had 'suspended' her soul in space so it could keep its clarity, and sense of permanence.

When Annie first came to work with me she told me that she felt almost utterly lifeless, as though her life force had, over the past eight years, finally just drained away. She could walk, albeit slowly, but felt as though her young, thirty year old body was almost paralysed.

Annie and I worked intently together over a number of weeks but Annie had a sense of trepidation about trusting the stirring of energy in her body. What if she trusted and was wrong? She couldn't bear being wrong.

Eight years prior to my meeting Annie, and to me having

151

the great privilege to work with her, she had been in a seriously abusive relationship. Her partner, she told me, had drained her of every last 'molecule' of her sense of self.

Then one day, as she was summoning some last vestige of energy to walk away from the relationship, she had an experience of vertigo which terrified her, and from that moment she had hardly slept.

Together she and I discovered the deep inherent logic behind her not sleeping; if she kept her eyes open she could ascertain that her world was not spinning out of control, as during the first terrifying attack of vertigo.

By the time Annie knocked at my door asking for my help, she was suffering not only chronic lack of sleep, attacks of vertigo, debilitating tinnitus, coeliac disease and anaemia, she also had cancer.

As Annie and I worked intently towards her goal, 'To have energy to be healthy and be as fresh as a daisy,' she had an Epiphany.

I was asking Annie to visualise something which I believed would lead to important information on her journey to her goal. And indeed this is exactly what happened, but not in the way anyone would ever imagine, which is the beauty and inherent wisdom of this kind of therapeutic work.

Annie said; 'I'm finding it really hard to make the image, the image just keeps disappearing.'

My next question was a stroke of genius and that genius came, not directly from me, but from the teachings and work of my great teacher and mentor David Grove.

I asked: 'And, when you are finding it really hard to make the image *how do you know* that you are finding it really hard?'

Annie responded immediately, her story pouring from her; 'This is important, to get the image right, and 'If' I try to do something important I will fail. I feel a failure. I feel I am no good. I feel I am not good enough. When something important has to be done, it has to be done correctly and I never trust myself to do it right. So, I don't try to do it.

If I do try I will fail!

So, I don't try for fear of failing!

At school and at college I was always hiding in the background.

At work I always wanted someone else to do whatever was important.

If I tried I believed I would fail.

So, I didn't try for fear of failing.'

I asked Annie, 'And when you have the feeling of not being good enough, and when you have a fear of failing whereabouts inside of you or around you do you have these feelings?'

Annie answered, a flow of consciousness, 'I always carry it around with me.

It's like a big heavy coat with a big heavy hood – it weighs me down – it makes me stoop. It exhausts me. The hood covers the whole of my head, I can barely see. The coat is black and heavy, heavy. It does have a bright red light shiny lining – like satin. But the black heavy coat and hood completely encase me and no one can see my bright light shininess. No one can see me; I'm like a stooped broken figure. The heaviness of it has built up over all the years; it has got heavier and heavier. I can never rest, even when I lie down the heaviness is so tiring, always so uncomfortable and exhausting. It makes me too tired to sleep. The weight of it is dragging me down and down it is crushing me. The pressure that it puts on me I can feel it physically as well as mentally, it is destroying the real me. I don't think anyone has ever seen the real me! Including me! I feel the real 'me' has been stifled – the real 'me' can never shine properly...'

As Annie and I engaged with the 'heavy coat', searching for the right solutions for her, she came to the realisation that this heavy burden of such self doubt and fear of failure had originated, sadly, from the beliefs of significant adults in the world outside of her home. They had 'burdened' Annie, during her childhood years, with their beliefs about her lack of ability.

The sadness for little Annie was that her brightness had been so dulled and shadowed and weighed down by the doubts of others. This is not a negative criticism of the adults' behaviour and attitudes towards Annie when she was a child, simply an important observation of the lack of knowledge and information that adults so often display when relating to children who are different.

I believe that Annie, as a small child, was using her brain very differently from the 'normal'. I understand that little Annie had truly profound thoughts, and saw the world in an unusual and distinctive way. A child with 'gifts'.

Annie faced the questions: 'Am I up to trusting myself to be successful? How can I know?'

What seemed like a complex dilemma for Annie was truly simple to resolve. Of course Annie had felt completely overwhelmed by such a massive obstacle, the burden of her fear of failure. The solution came to her. In one defining moment she let it go. She let go the fear that had so overwhelmed her throughout her life in the moment that she validated, with consummate passion, her own intelligence and differences. And I was so privileged to truly witness that moment for her and with her. In her mind, and with the assistance of the clarity and resourcefulness of her 'soul' or true identity Annie turned the heavy, heavy coat with the hood, to vapour and banished the weight of the burden she had carried nearly her entire life.

We can relate to Annie's own unique metaphor of transforming this burden to vapour, when, after all, the weight of her fear had originated in the 'hot air' beliefs from others about little Annie's lack of capabilities!

Annie began, in that defining moment to accept her own brightness.

Annie is a lesson to us all.

Her energy is coming back, she is no longer anaemic, she sleeps better now, and her scan results are clear. Annie and I will continue a while longer to work together.

Annie recently told me of a mysterious and happy event. She had gone for a walk and as she walked she asked her unconscious to give her a 'sign' about her goal and how close she could be to getting there. If you remember her goal is 'to have energy to be healthy and be as fresh as a daisy'.

As she asked for a sign Annie instantly saw a woodpecker in its nest, something she had longed to see, but never had.

I asked what was important to her about seeing the woodpecker and Annie answered vibrantly, 'The nest is important and oh, the amazing sound.'

'What kind of a sound is that amazing sound?' I asked. Annie answered immediately; 'Ki, Ki, Ki.'

We looked up the word 'Ki' – and very simplistically it means energy!

Annie will continue to bring the purity of gold to her thoughts...

Libby's Story.

If I look up to the stars I will smile, if I keep looking down I will frown.

— *Libby Bolton*

I have journeyed with Libby for one hundred and twenty days. She is such an inspiration.

Libby tells you her story, she wrote it for me and sent it in the post. It was brilliant to open, neatly hand-written on sheets of pale blue paper.

'My name is Libby and I am fifty-three years old. I consider myself to be a nice person. You see, I had to learn to love myself; my childhood was so hard, I never ever felt loved. Then my first husband was a control freak. For thirteen years I just existed. I was beaten up, and I was also put down with every word he ever spoke to me.

When I finally got out of that I made a promise to myself to trust only in myself.

Life on the outside got easier, but on the inside I was crying and crying all the time.

By 1999 my parents were dead and by 2006 I had lost my brother and my sister.

I had lovely people beside me, my second husband and my three children. And yet I still felt the crying and crying going on and on inside me.

From 2006 I threw myself into work, doing two part time jobs and wedding buffets at weekends. All this was just activity, no time for reflection, just work keeping me on my feet, keeping me constantly busy and so stopping me from thinking about the past. But you see I know that this was just 'papering over the cracks', and not bringing any kind of healing for me to my past, not helping me move on into what I had, in the present a good life with my lovely husband and my lovely children. I just kept on working I just kept on going to try to save me from the pain of thinking of the years gone by.

Then in February 2010 I was diagnosed with alopecia and within eight weeks I was totally, totally bald.

I was completely devastated. I did not have any faith in the doctors. Why should I? They were not helpful.

I read about an alopecia club in the town where I live and I thought: 'If I go along maybe they, or someone could help me…' I went along and I told the group that I do not trust people easily. I made a friend and I was put in contact with Sally Stubbs.

But here I was having to think about putting my trust in a complete stranger. Could I trust Sally to help?

But what more did I have to lose; I mean I'd lost all my hair, which is a devastating thing, to lose all your hair.
A leaflet arrived with Sally's course which said 'You can grow your own hair'.

I thought, if only I could. I thought, if I do this one hundred and twenty day course what will happen? Well this is what happened. On May 15th 2010 I made my mind up to do the course. I listened every day, I worked on my journal, I listened to the stories and to the relaxations, and very soon I got to feel really focused and wanting to do it. And, within two weeks I noticed changes like my nails were stronger, which I strangely knew meant an emotional change and strengthening for me and there were tiny little hairs on my bald head.

Then I thought if I continue, if I just trust in Sally's work to help me, something good can continue to happen for me. And wow, by the ninth part of my course, which was on day eighty one, I really did understand the importance of trust. I also knew by then that every single hair I had lost represented every pain that I had ever felt and suffered. Yes, that's right. I knew that I had suffered thousands of pains.

My emotional pain has healed now, it's like it has mysteriously been acknowledged, like my pains have been witnessed or respected and so they are gone.

When I started the course I had some edible seeds, which I had hoped against hope would help my hair to grow if I ate them. I took those seeds and planted them in a plant pot, they became a kind of symbol for me, if the seeds grow so will my hair. Sally taught me a lot about belief on her course. I have this thought now which is, 'if I believe then I will achieve.' And yes, the plant pot is full of lovely purple flowers, and yes, my head is full of lovely hair.

The course is like an exciting journey, a bit like the *Matrix* film for me, I listened to the course a couple of times and I was hooked, I was excited I wanted to know and learn and achieve more and more. I find myself smiling a lot of the time. I can now tell myself If I look up to the stars I will smile, if I keep looking down I will frown.

I find myself helping other people with my knowledge from Sally's course. I'd like to tell you one of my stories, about an elderly gentleman who I work with. He is eighty-nine and he is crippled with arthritis, although he can use his walking frame. He used to play the trumpet in a band, a man full of music and rhythm. He loves the rock and roll years and he loved to dance. But he told me that he can't walk, let alone dance, anymore. I found myself saying to him, 'Does your brain want to dance but your body believes it can't?' He said 'Yes, that's right'. I replied, 'Focus your mind that you can get up and dance…' And he got up, with a little help, and then he did dance; he rocked to 'Rock Around the Clock'. How brilliant is that? As he sat down he cried tears of absolute joy.'

Libby will continue to bring the purity of gold to her thoughts…

Quotes to continue to bring the purity of gold to your thoughts...

These quotes will uplift and enhance your mood when you are feeling miserable, dejected, down in the dumps, despondent, worried, concerned, nervous, or fretful.

Gold is a chemical element with the symbol Au from the Latin *aurum* meaning 'shining dawn'. Gold is the most dense and flexible pure metal known.

'If...' quotes and stories for the gold of your thoughts enable you to bring flexibility and certainty to your thoughts, and also the clear and expansive dawning of new thoughts for you.

'If I knew for certain that I should die next week, I would still be able to sit at my desk all week and study with perfect equanimity, for I know now that life and death make a meaningful whole.'

— *Etty Hillesum*

'If some men died and others did not, death would indeed be a most mortifying evil.'

— *Jean De La Bruyere*

'If your time ain't come not even a doctor can kill you.'

— *American proverb*

'If thou expect death as a friend, prepare to entertain it; if thou expect death as an enemy, prepare to overcome it; death has no advantage, except when it comes as a stranger.'

— *Francis Quarles*

'If you would behold the spirit of death, open your heart wide unto the body of life. For life and death are one, even as the river and sea are one.'

— *Kahlil Gibran*

'If you're not ready to die, then how can you live?'
— *Charles de Lint*

'If what the heart approves conforms to proper patterns, then even if one's desires are many, what harm would they be to good order?'
— *Xun Zi*

'If you spend too much time thinking about a thing, you'll never get it done.'
— *Bruce Lee*

'If you want to reach a goal, you must "see the reaching" in your own mind before you actually arrive at your goal.'
— *Zig Ziglar*

If you do what you've always done, you'll get what you've always gotten.'
— *Tony Robbins*

'If you wish to achieve worthwhile things in your personal and career life, you must become a worthwhile person in your own self-development.'

— *Brian Tracy*

'If you pursue good with labour, the labour passes away but the good remains; if you pursue evil with pleasure, the pleasure passes away and the evil remains.'

— *Cicero*

'If we were to wake up some morning and find that everyone was the same race, creed and colour, we would find some other cause for prejudice by noon.'

— *George Aiken*

'If a man be gracious and courteous to strangers, it shows he is a citizen of the world.'

— *Francis Bacon*

'If a person loves only one other person and is indifferent to all others, his love is not love but a symbiotic attachment, or an enlarged egotism.'

— *Erich Fromm*

'If you want to achieve excellence, you can get there today. As of this second, quit doing less-than-excellent work.'

— *Thomas J. Watson*

'If you want to succeed in the world you must make your own opportunities as you go on. The man who waits for some seventh wave to toss him on dry land will find that the seventh wave is a long time a-coming. You can commit no greater folly than to sit by the road side until someone comes along and invites you to ride with him to wealth or influence.'

— *John B. Gough*

'If we could have a little patience, we should escape much mortification; time takes away as much as it gives.'

— *Marquis De Sevigne*

'If you can dream it, you can do it.'

— *Walt Disney*

'If a man takes no thought about what is distant, he will find sorrow near at hand.'

— *Confucius*

'If you accept the expectations of others, especially negative ones, then you never will change the outcome.'

— *Michael Jordan*

'If boyhood and youth are but vanity, must it not be our ambition to become men?'

— *Vincent van Gogh*

'If you believe you can, you probably can. If you believe you won t, you most assuredly won't. Belief is the ignition switch that gets you off the launching pad.'

— *Denis Waitley*

If you would have people speak well of you, then do not speak well of yourself.'

— *Blaise Pascal*

'If you pull one pig by the tail all the rest squeak.'

— *Dutch proverb*

'If there were no fault, there would be no pardon.'

— *Egyptian proverb*

'If you paint in your mind a picture of bright and happy expectations, you put yourself into a condition conducive to your goal.'

— *Norman Vincent Peale*

'If you don't set a baseline standard for what you'll accept in life, you'll find it's easy to slip into behaviors and attitudes or a quality of life that's far below what you deserve.'

— *Anthony Robbins*

'If you desire many things, many things will seem few.'

— *Benjamin Franklin*

'If a man will begin with certainties, he shall end in doubts; but if he will be content to begin with doubts he shall end in certainties.'

— *Sir Francis Bacon*

'If there exists no possibility of failure, then victory is meaningless.'

— Robert H. Schuller

'If you are idle, be not solitary; if you are solitary, be not idle.'

— Samuel Johnson

'If you do not ask the right questions, you do not get the right answers. A question asked in the right way often points to its own answer. Asking questions is the A-B-C of diagnosis. Only the inquiring mind solves problems.'

— Edward Hodnett

'If you change the way you look at things, the things you look at change.'

— Wayne Dyer

'If you would live innocently, seek solitude.'

— Publilius Syrus

'If you wish to appear agreeable in society, you must consent to be taught many things which you know already.'

— *Johann Kaspar Lavater*

'If thou are a master, be sometimes blind; if a servant, sometimes deaf.'

— *Thomas Fuller*

'If you want to achieve your dreams, you must follow them, and the best way to follow them is not to think about wanting to be very rich, but to think about doing something that you really want to do.'

— *Jackie Collins*

'If a man does his best, what else is there?'

— *General George S. Patton*

'If there is a God, he's a great mathematician.'

— *Paul Dirac*

'If you would marry suitably, marry your equal.'

— *Ovid*

'If I had my life over again I should form the habit of nightly composing myself to thoughts of death. I would practice, as it were, the remembrance of death. There is no other practice which so intensifies life. Death, when it approaches, ought not to take one by surprise. It should be part of the full expectancy of life. Without an ever-present sense of death life is insipid. You might as well live on the whites of eggs.'

— *Muriel Spark*

'If you would persuade, you must appeal to interest rather than intellect.'

— *Benjamin Franklin*

'If you would convince a man that he does wrong, do right. Men will believe what they see.'

— *Henry David Thoreau*

'If you want your life to be more rewarding, you have to change the way you think.'

— *Oprah Winfrey*

'If you do not tell the truth about yourself you cannot tell it about other people.'

— Virginia Woolf

'If we take care of the moments, the years will take care of themselves.'

— Maria Edgeworth

'If you think taking care of yourself is selfish, change your mind. If you don't, you're simply ducking your responsibilities.'

— Ann Richards

'If a man withdraws his mind from the love of beauty, and applies it as sincerely to the love of the virtuous; if, in serving his parents, he can exert his utmost strength; if, in serving his prince, he can devote his life; if in his intercourse with his friends, his words are sincere – although men say that he has not learned, I will certainly say that he has.'

— Confucius

'If we say a little it is easy to add, but having said too much it is hard to withdraw and never can it be done so quickly as to hinder the harm of our success.'

— Saint Francis de Sales

'If one has no vanity in this life of ours, there is no sufficient reason for living.'

— *Leo Tolstoy*

'If you have embraced a creed which appears to be free from the ordinary dirtiness of politics – a creed from which you yourself cannot expect to draw any material advantage – surely that proves that you are in the right?'

— *George Orwell*

'If you make yourself more than just a man, if you devote yourself to an ideal, you become something else entirely.'

— *Henri Ducard (Batman Begins)*

'If you gaze long into an abyss, the abyss will gaze back into you.'

— *Friedrich Nietzsche*

'If we will be quiet and ready enough, we shall find compensation in every disappointment.'

— *Henry David Thoreau*

'If you believe in fate, believe in it, at least, for your good.'
— *Ralph Waldo Emerson*

'If there were no God, there would be no Atheists.'
— *G. K. Chesterton*

'If one wishes to form a true estimate of the full grandeur
of religion, one must keep in mind what it undertakes to do
for men. It gives them information about the source and
origin of the universe, it assures them of protection and
final happiness amid the changing vicissitudes of life, and it
guides their thoughts and motions by means of precepts
which are backed by the whole force of its authority.'
— *Sigmund Freud*

'If you can't change your fate, change your attitude.'
— *Amy Tan*

'If you want to live a happy life, tie it to a goal, not to people
or objects.'
— *Albert Einstein*

'If there were no God, it would be necessary to invent him.'
— *Voltaire*

'If prayer is us speaking to God, then intuition is God speaking to us.'
— *Wayne Dyer*

'If the whole universe has no meaning, we should never have found out that it has no meaning: just as, if there were no light in the universe and therefore no creatures with eyes, we should never know it was dark. Dark would be without meaning.'
— *C. S. Lewis*

'If you desire faith, then you have faith enough.'
— *Elizabeth Barrett Browning*

'If the believers of the present-day religions would earnestly try to think and act in the spirit of the founders of these religions then no hostility on the basis of religion would exist among the followers of the different faiths. Even the conflicts and the realm of religion would be exposed as insignificant.'
— *Albert Einstein*

'If you gaze at a single leaf on a single tree, you do not see the other leaves. If you face the tree with no intention and do not fix your eyes on a single leaf, then you will see all the many leaves. If your mind is preoccupied with one leaf, you do not see the others, if you do not set your attention on one; you will see hundreds and thousands of leaves.'

— *Yagyu Munenori*

'If you get simple beauty and naught else, you get about the best thing God invents.'

— *Robert Browning*

'If God created us in his own image, we have more than reciprocated.'

— *Voltaire*

'If I am capable of grasping God objectively, I do not believe, but precisely because I cannot do this I must believe.'

— *Soren Kierkegaard*

'If the stars should appear but one night every thousand years how man would marvel and stare.'

— *Ralph Waldo Emerson*

'If moderation is a fault, then indifference is a crime.'
— *Georg C. Lichtenberg*

'If goodness were only a theory, it were a pity it should be lost to the world. There are a number of things, the idea of which is a clear gain to the mind. Let people, for instance, rail at friendship, genius, freedom, as long as they will – the very names of these despised qualities are better than anything else that could be substituted for them, and embalm even the most envenomed satire against them.'
— *William Hazlitt*

'If all mankind were suddenly to practice honesty, many thousands of people would be sure to starve.'
— *Georg C. Lichtenberg*

'If pleasure was not followed by pain, who would forbear it?'
— *Samuel Johnson*

'If there ever could be a justifiable war in the name of and for humanity, a war against Germany, to prevent the wanton persecution of a whole race, would be completely justified. But I do not believe in any war. A discussion of the pros and cons of such a war is therefore outside my horizon or province.'
— *Mohandas Gandhi*

'If the tongue had not been framed for articulation, man would still be a beast in the forest.'

— *Ralph Waldo Emerson*

'If mankind minus one were of one opinion, then mankind is no more justified in silencing the one than the one – if he had the power – would be justified in silencing mankind.'

— *John Stuart Mill*

'If man does find the solution for world peace it will be the most revolutionary reversal of his record we have ever known.'

— *George C. Marshall*

'If you tell the truth you don't have to remember anything.'

— *Mark Twain*

'If a man is offered a fact which goes against his instincts, he will scrutinize it closely, and unless the evidence is overwhelming, he will refuse to believe it. If, on the other hand, he is offered something which affords a reason for acting in accordance to his instincts, he will accept it even on the slightest evidence. The origin of myths is explained in this way.'

— *Bertrand Russell*

'If we want everything to remain as it is, it will be necessary for everything to change.'
— *Giuseppe Tomasi Di Lampedusa*

'If we are to go forward, we must go back and rediscover those precious values – that all reality hinges on moral foundations and that all reality has spiritual control.'
— *Martin Luther King, Jr.*

'If history repeats itself, and the unexpected always happens, how incapable must Man be of learning from experience.'
— *George Bernard Shaw*

'If nobody spoke unless he had something to say, the human race would very soon lose the use of speech.'
— *W. Somerset Maugham*

'If all the year were playing holidays; To sport would be as tedious as to work.'
— *William Shakespeare (Henry IV, Part I)*

'If you want to be respected, you must respect yourself.'

— *Spanish proverb*

'If one speaks or acts with a cruel mind, misery follows, as the cart follows the horse... If one speaks or acts with a pure mind, happiness follows, as a shadow follows its source.'

— *The Dhammapada*

'If we could see the miracle of a single flower clearly, our whole life would change.'

— *Buddha*

'If I am not for myself, who will be for me? If I am not for others, what am I? And if not now, when?'

— *Rabbi Hillel*

'If we aren't capable of being hurt we aren't capable of feeling joy.'

— *Madeleine L'Engle*

'If you could be God's worst enemy or nothing, which would you choose?'

— *Chuck Palahniuk (Fight Club)*

'If you were to destroy in mankind the belief in immortality, not only love but every living force maintaining the life of the world would at once be dried up.'

— *Fyodor Dostoevsky (The Brothers Karamazov)*

'If one is forever cautious, can one remain a human being?'

— *Alexander Solzhenitsyn*

'If you don't get what you want, you suffer; if you get what you don't want, you suffer; even when you get exactly what you want, you still suffer because you can't hold on to it forever.'

— *Dan Millman*

'If you want to see the true measure of a man, watch how he treats his inferiors, not his equals.'

— *J. K. Rowling*

'If honour were profitable, everybody would be honourable.'

— *Thomas More*

'If God gives you a watch, are you honouring Him more by asking Him what time it is or by simply consulting the watch?'

— *A. W. Tozer*

'If triangles made a god, they would give him three sides.'

— *Charles De Montesquieu*

'If by any possibility the existence of a power superior to, and independent of, nature shall be demonstrated, there will then be time enough to kneel. Until then, let us stand erect.'

— *Robert G. Ingersol*

'If men could regard the events of their own lives with more open minds, they would frequently discover that they did not really desire the things they failed to obtain.'

— *Andre Maurois*

'If you don't get lost, there's a chance you may never be found.'

— *Anonymous*

'If we really think about it, God exists for any single individual who puts his trust in Him, not for the whole of humanity, with its laws, its organizations, and its violence. Humanity is the demon which God does not succeed in destroying.'

— *Salvatore Satta*

'If you resist reading what you disagree with, how will you ever acquire deeper insights into what you believe? The things most worth reading are precisely those that challenge our convictions.'

— *Anonymous*

'If you cannot find the truth right where you are, where else do you expect to find it?'

— *Dogan*

'If a thousand old beliefs were ruined in our march to truth we must still march on.'

— *Stopford Brooke*

'If wisdom and diamonds grew on the same tree we could soon tell how much men loved wisdom.'

— Lemeul K. Washburn

'If we do not end war – war will end us. Everybody says that, millions of people believe it, and nobody does anything.'

— H. G. Wells (Things to Come)

'If it were proved to me that in making war, my ideal had a chance of being realized, I would still say 'no' to war. For one does not create a human society on mounds of corpses.'

— Louis Lecoin

'If we cannot be happy and powerful and prey on others, we invent conscience and prey on ourselves.'

— Elbert Hubbard

'If frugality were established in the state, and if our expenses were laid out to meet needs rather than superfluities of life, there might be fewer wants, and even fewer pleasures, but infinitely more happiness.'

— Oliver Goldsmith

'If you prick us do we not bleed? If you tickle us do we not laugh? If you poison us do we not die? And if you wrong us shall we not revenge?'

— *William Shakespeare (Merchant of Venice)*

'If you only have a hammer, you tend to see every problem as a nail.'

— *Abraham Maslow*

'If you plan on being anything less than you are capable of being, you will probably be unhappy all the days of your life.'

— *Abraham Maslow*

'If they want peace, nations should avoid the pin-pricks that precede cannon shots.'

— *Napoleon Bonaparte*

'If there be no enemy there's no fight. If no fight, no victory and if no victory there is no crown.'

— *Thomas Carlyle*

'If we justify war, it is because all peoples always justify the traits of which they find themselves possessed, not because war will bear an objective examination of its merits.'

— *Ruth Benedict*

'If everyone demanded peace instead of another television set, then there'd be peace.'

— *John Lennon*

'If you know the enemy and know yourself you need not fear the results of a hundred battles.'

— *Sun Tzu*

'If we are to teach real peace in this world, and if we are to carry on a real war against war, we shall have to begin with the children.'

— *Mohandas Gandhi*

'If you're not part of the solution, you're part of the precipitate.'

— *Henry J. Tillman*

'If you want peace, stop fighting. If you want peace of mind, stop fighting with your thoughts.'

— Peter McWilliams

'If you ain't never pick up the sword, you ain't never have to worry about fallin' on it.'

— Meldrick Lewis

'If any foreign minister begins to defend to the death a 'peace conference,' you can be sure his government has already placed its orders for new battleships and airplanes.'

— Joseph Stalin

'If you look for truth, you may find comfort in the end; if you look for comfort you will not get either comfort or truth only soft soap and wishful thinking to begin, and in the end, despair.'

— C. S. Lewis

'If some persons died, and others did not die, death would be a terrible affliction.'

— *Jean de La Bruyere*

'If we catch a glimpse of freedom, we wish to possess it; if we catch a glimpse of death, we want nothing to do with it. One we cannot have, the other we cannot avoid.'

— *Jeremy Preston Johnson*

'If you don't know how to die, don't worry; Nature will tell you what to do on the spot, fully and adequately. She will do this job perfectly for you; don't bother your head about it.'

— *Michel Eyquem de Montaigne*

'If man were immortal he could be perfectly sure of seeing the day when everything in which he had trusted should betray his trust, and, in short, of coming eventually to hopeless misery. He would break down, at last, as every good fortune, as every dynasty, as every civilization does. In place of this we have death.'

— *Charles Sanders Pierce*

'If I am killed, I can die but once; but to live in constant dread of it, is to die over and over again.'

— *Abraham Lincoln*

'If I think more about death than some other people, it is probably because I love life more than they do.'

— *Angelina Jolie*

'If my decomposing carcass helps nourish the roots of a juniper tree or the wings of a vulture – that is immortality enough for me. And as much as anyone deserves.'

— *Edward Abbey*

'If you seek, how is that different from pursuing sound and form? If you don't seek, how are you different from earth, wood, or stone? You must seek without seeking.'

— *Fo Yan*

'If you want to be successful, it's just this simple. Know what you are doing. Love what you are doing. And believe in what you are doing.'

— *Will Rogers*

'If you do not hope, you will not find what is beyond your hopes.'
— St. Clement of Alexandria

My Courses
I wrote them for you.

I wrote them for you because my dream for you is that you are able to go as far as you want and need in your own unique way. I do this because I have experienced the hurt, the pain, the frustrations and the despair, and many years ago I travelled my own 'healing' journey. Since my healing journey, since discovering my own inner resources the most amazing things have happened and continue to happen in my life. In my younger years I was not heard, but unlike Laura, who 'stood on her feet' to speak, I stopped speaking; I hid in silence. After my healing journey I rediscovered my own voice and the elegance of its truth.

My courses are not prescriptive, they are not rigid and they are not authoritarian, they cannot be, because your solutions and resolutions to heal your pains, bewilderment or concerns are and will be absolutely unique to you. My language is clean and precise.

You discover your own solutions and you access your own inner unique strengths and resources.

During my courses I assist you to pause at cross roads so you can read the right signs, the right way to go, for yourself.

In my courses I approach you carefully, as if you were someone who is lost, someone who is off course. I assist you to know that you do, deep down unconsciously, know your own way home and I walk beside as you travel, as you find your path to your home.

My courses have assignments; each assignment takes five or ten minutes a day for ten days.

First assignment takes ten days to set your Goal, hone your goal, and discover the deeper purposes for yourself to attain your goal.

Second assignment is about establishing motivation – about creating within an intense desire to break free of malaise that confounds success.

Third assignment is about beliefs, about creating a childlike willingness to suspend disbeliefs, and one by one letting go of negative beliefs that are blockages to total success and goal achieving.

Fourth assignment is future pacing – one step at a time - associating more and more completely with your goal state and moving forward into a problem free state. Moving forward then backward to check out and dissolve or resolve any blocks to success.

Then there are my Stories, taking twenty to twenty five minutes a day to listen to comfortably and take your own inner heroes journey. The hero's journey starts at the beginning with a problem to solve, obstacles to triumph over, a need to overcome an inner battle, the need to bring an inner peace, and the discovery of unique inner solutions and resolutions to achieve triumph and success.

My CD Courses available on CD and Mp3 downloads.

40 day courses – plus three month support.

Gain Self Confidence and Self Esteem
Discover exactly where and when you need Self Confidence for yourself. Learn exactly what you need to learn and to develop for you in your life. Find out how you can begin to validate yourself.

Sleep Well
Discover exactly what it is that is stopping you from sleeping well, sometimes this can be about

worrying. If so, you will discover your own solutions to your worries. Sometimes lack of sleep has become habituated because of a time in life when sleeping deeply was not appropriate. For example: when we have a new baby, or when someone is very unwell and many other reasons. Learn during my course that your mind and brain can now accept that is safe and right for you to sleep well.

Resolve Your Relationship problems

I am particularly passionate about this course, as I would like to think that we can live in harmony with our self and with others in our life. My course assists you to relate better within your self and to your self. My course assists you to learn how to relate with others differently, allows you to take one step into the world of another and bring understanding between you and them.

Resolve Your Upset and Nervous Stomach

I developed this course because a lot of people would come to me and talk about having an upset, nervous stomach. This decidedly uncomfortable feeling was so often triggered by things in life such as taking exams or tests, going for interviews and so on. This course will assist you to access inner resources and strengths in such a way as for you to feel stable and comfortable no matter what is happening in your life. However if you do at anytime need the adrenalin rush to run away or to 'fight' then of course this will happen for you naturally and healthily.

Kick Your Annoying Habits

I wrote this course thinking of you perhaps with nail biting or hair twiddling, or a need to check things several times. Anything that you know is an annoying habit and therefore is time wasting for you.
Habits that are constructive are great as they save us time. Like, you can habitually tie your shoe laces and your mind is free to take time to think of other things.
This course is about you kicking an annoying habit that is not constructive or time saving for you.

Resolve Stress

Stress is a huge subject; in 2007-2008, 442, 000 people in Britain suffered with work related stress. We feel stressed and agitated from a number of causes including pressure and lack of time. My course assists you to learn how to deal with pressures appropriately and comfortably. My course assists you to relate to time, for example deadlines at work, family and home commitments with a balanced ease and suitability for your needs.

Resolve Your Anger

Another one of my courses that I am particularly passionate about, because most of my heroes are reformists who use anger constructively to bring about reform. Anger can be righteous and evolutionary when used constructively. I'd like to see you using your anger to bring change to something in life that you know is wrong. My course will assist you to heal the wrong that you suffered and, if you choose, enable you to use righteous anger appropriately.

Resolve Your Phobia

A phobia response is an unnatural fear response, and will not always make sense. For example, if you are phobic of spiders, in the UK this will not make sense to you, as spiders in the UK are not toxic. If you are phobic of flying, your brain will try to make sense that this is unnatural and dangerous to be hurling along at over 30, 000.000 feet in the air. And yet it won't fully make sense as there are more deaths from crossing the road than from flying. Any phobia you may suffer you will discover the lack of sense. My course assists your mind to understand the phobic response and then to feel and be calm no matter what phobia you have been experiencing.

You Will lose Weight

I believe that you have been waiting long enough to lose your weight and to become slim, toned and healthy. You are reading this because you have probably tried and tried so many ways to lose weight. My course assists you to discover exactly what has been stopping you from being successful, to discover, resolve and, at last, free yourself from the blocks to your success.

Stop Smoking Now!
My course ensures that you become so totally focused on your goal and on your success and the purposes of your goal whatever they are for you, maybe your health, maybe the health of a loved one, finance and so on. You will become so motivated, you will have such total belief that soon you will totally forget about that old habit.

Resolve Sickness In Pregnancy
I have total belief that if just one woman on the planet can have a healthy and happy pregnancy then all woman can. I've gathered information over more than twenty years to be able to put into this course how women who have a healthy happy pregnancy do it. I wish you health and happiness and a comfortable pregnancy and a huge welcome to your baby.

120 day course – plus four months support

You Can Grow Your Own Hair!
I developed this course over a number of years, as I had suffered with alopecia. I successfully grew my own hair, with no recurrence of loss. If I can do this, so can you.

Coming Soon

Have a Comfortable and Natural Menopause
A Highway to Happiness
Resolve Your Depression
Cure Your Hay Fever

www.sally-stubbs.com

In 1982 Sally Stubbs qualified as a Clinical Hypnotherapist and Licensed Psychotherapist and went into full time practice in Cumbria. From 1994-1997 she was Consultant to the Juvenile Justice team in Cumbria, assisting teenagers (14-17 year olds) to stop offending. She has worked for almost three decades as a psychotherapist.